Occasional Paper 99

Restoration: Is It Acceptable?

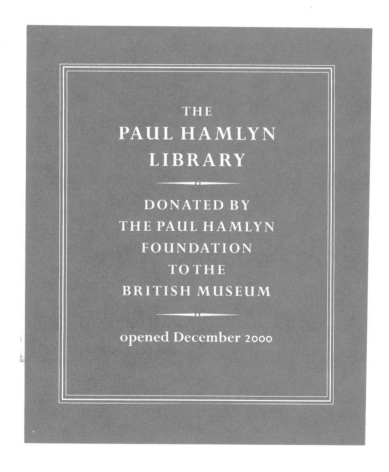

edited by Andrew Oddy

Department of Conservation 1994

BRITISH MUSEUM OCCASIONAL PAPERS

Publishers: The British Museum
                               Great Russell Street
                               London WC1B 3DG

Production Editor: Josephine Turquet
Typing: Brenda Burr
                               Kim Havercroft
                               Vivienne Tremain

Distributors: British Museum Press
                               46 Bloomsbury Street
                               London WC1B 3QQ

Front Cover: Head of the Lansdowne *Herakles*
from the J Paul Getty Museum, Malibu, California

Occasional Paper No. 99, 1994:
Restoration - Is It Acceptable?

Edited by Andrew Oddy

ISBN 0 86159 099 6
ISSN 0142 4815

Orders should be sent to British Museum Press.
Cheques and postal orders should be made payable to
British Museum Publications Ltd and sent to
46 Bloomsbury Street, London WC1B 3QQ.
Access, American Express, Barclaycard and Visa cards are accepted.

Printed and bound by GBA Reprographics Ltd.

CONTENTS

FOREWORD

Codes of practice and ethical conduct are currently very topical in all walks of life. The concept of giving satisfaction is, however, not new, but the concept of setting targets for achievement is. In conservation the problem is not so simple, as the targets are as variable as the clients. Invisible restoration will be the goal of one customer, but anathema to the next. Furthermore, the outcome of treatment is, these days, likely to be constrained by the budget available to pay for the work. And this is equally as true in many museums as in the private sector.

The aim of this conference is to explore attitudes to restoration, and the title of the meeting, *Restoration - is it acceptable*? was deliberately framed as a question. But first the contributors had to ask themselves two supplementary questions: what is meant by restoration, and, acceptable to whom?

Contributions have been selected and solicited from as many disciplines of conservation as possible, from computers to carpets, pianos to paintings, and mosaics to murals, and the authors were asked to address the various dilemmas facing conservators, curators and collectors in the display and interpretation of 'museum' objects. Among the problems to be discussed are invisible restoration, the running of machinery and clocks, and the introduction of replica components.

Whether we have achieved our main 'aim' is for you to judge, but we also have a hidden agenda and that is to explore the applicability of 'codes of practice'. Many of these have been cited by the various authors, but do we all agree on their universal applicability? In my opinion, the 'ideal' code of practice should be very simple and very short. It should raise issues, but not pontificate on the solutions to problems; it should offer guidelines, without rigorously constraining. And if we can avoid the use of the word 'ethics', so much the better.

Andrew Oddy
July 1994

RESTORATION - IS IT ACCEPTABLE?

Andrew Oddy

Department of Conservation, The British Museum, London, WC1B 3DG

The title of this symposium was deliberately phrased as a question, but one which itself poses two more questions - what is meant by restoration, and, acceptable to whom? It is the purpose of this introductory paper to examine these two questions.

The Shorter Oxford English Dictionary[1] defines restoration as 'the action of restoring to a former state or position'. This definition clearly distinguishes 'restoration' from 'conservation', as it is understood in the museum world. In fact, 'restoration' is one stage of the conservation process, which usually consists of three steps: cleaning, stabilisation, and restoration. But within this final stage there are a multitude of possibilities from reassembly of existing fragments, through reassembly and infilling, to reassembly, infilling and invisible retouching. Within different conservation disciplines, and within different institutions dealing with similar material, and sometimes even within a single institution, there are different ethical approaches to one or more of these stages. Thus, although this symposium is mainly concerned with restoration, it might be instructive to look briefly at cleaning and stabilisation.

Cleaning is generally understood as the revelation of detail by the removal of surface dirt and concretion. But is it always right (ethically acceptable) to remove surface dirt? What if it relates to the use to which the object was put? What if it has accumulated while the object was in use, but is incidental to the actual use? And what if the deposit is actually derived from the object itself?

Deposits relating to the original use of the object are usually known as 'ethnographical dirt' and may consist of food remains in vessels, wax or oil in lamps, traces of religious offerings on altars or images, or simply traces of animal secretions on horse harness for instance. A classic example is the blood stain on the shirt which President Lincoln was wearing when he was assassinated. In the past, all these stains and deposits would have been removed without question. Today, none of them would be.

There is no question, however, about the removal of museum dirt, that is dirt which has accumulated on an object since it was collected, but there is every reason to question the removal of deposits which accumulated as a result of the object being used for its original purpose.

More problematic is the removal of incidental dirt - the cleaning of pictures from churches where candles are regularly burnt is an example. Most conservators would not have any qualms about this, but is this really restoration? If an object is still in use for its original purpose, are acts of maintenance really 'restoration', or are they really 'repair'? Take, for instance, a gilded image in a place of worship. As time progresses the gilding will become dull and worn and the question of regilding will arise. For an object still in use this is a natural development. For an object which has been moved to a museum, regilding should never be carried out.

For objects still in use for their original purpose, the English language tends to use the word 'repair' for utilitarian objects and the word 'restoration' for decorative/religious art, but the difference is illusory. However, cleaning of objects still in use is not governed by the museum ethical code (whatever that is), but rather by the desires of the owner(s) or user(s).

Finally, there is the question of removal of deposits which are part of the object, of which the best known examples are corrosion products on metals and alteration products on glass. Can it ever be right to remove corrosion products; there can be no question but that this action compromises the integrity of the object and is irreversible? The UKIC *Guidance for Conservation Practice* avoids the issue by saying that 'nothing should be removed from an object without sufficient evidence that it is not part of the original condition of the object'. The 'operative' word here is condition, and, hence, the removal of corrosion products is ethically acceptable to UKIC. And if corrosion products were never removed, how much poorer would be our appreciation of ancient art and craftsmanship?

This brief discussion of cleaning leads naturally to the subject of stabilisation, although, for some objects, stabilisation will precede cleaning because of their fragile condition.

Stabilisation is the act of arresting active decay and of preventing it from reoccurring. Thus, it may be non-interventive and consist only of establishing 'correct' environmental conditions, or it may be interventive and consist, for instance, of the removal of soluble salts from porous ceramics. It may consist of both approaches, as when bronze disease is treated chemically and then the bronze is stored in a controlled atmosphere.

No conservator or curator would see the provision of the 'correct' environmental conditions as anything other than essential, but environmental control *is* being questioned by increasing numbers of museum directors and administrators on the grounds of cost. This debate is not a subject for this conference, but suffice it to say that conservators have not always helped the situation by specifying impossibly 'tight' environmental conditions for objects which will not be at risk from a more relaxed approach.

Stabilisation may, however, compromise the integrity of the object. Thus, soluble salts which cause the decay of limestone may have been an original component of the stone. Should they be removed? And what about the addition of chemicals by the conservator as part of the stabilisation process?

Consolidation of fragile objects with synthetic resins is widespread, but what about the addition of consolidants which may be indistinguishable from the original materials of construction, such as the impregnation of limestone with lime-water? Are these treatments ethically acceptable? They are usually irreversible, but so is the complete removal of synthetic resin, however soluble it may remain!

The discussion so far has been mainly concerned with the stages of conservation which precede 'restoration'. Restoration itself can involve:

i   joining together of existing fragments;
ii   partial or complete infilling of missing areas;
iii   reshaping distorted objects;
iv   in-painting of joins between fragments and of 'restored' areas;
v   the construction of a conservation mount to safeguard the object both in storage and on display.

Many conservators would not consider the joining of original fragments as restoration, nor would they consider it as controversial. However, there are instances where this is not the case. Joining metals by soldering is irreversible and will alter the structure of the metal adjacent to the join. Nevertheless, soldering is sometimes acceptable, and may be the only way to join thin metal without making the join very obvious by using an adhesive in conjunction with the use of backing strips of fibreglass. Soldering, however, should be the method of last resort and be fully documented.

The conservation of organic objects is another field where the choice of adhesives is important in order to distinguish in the future between original manufacture, possible later repair, and museum restoration. Plant and animal extracts should normally be avoided for this reason.

One procedure frequently used in the past when joining fragments has been the trimming or filing of adjacent surfaces. This has usually been necessary when an object has been restored from many fragments and towards the end of the process the pieces will not fit into the spaces available. Examples are the first restoration of the Portland Vase in 1845 (Williams 1989, 17; Smith 1992, 56) and the Sutton Hoo helmet reconstruction in the 1940s. The use of minimal quantities of modern adhesives in the hands of skilled conservators has rendered the filing of joins a procedure of the past.

If joining is not normally controversial, gap filling may be. The first question to ask is whether it is necessary. Is the gap-fill carried out to strengthen the object or is it largely carried out for aesthetic reasons? Gap filling for strength or stability of the object is often necessary, particularly with ceramics, but is it always necessary to carry this process to completion? In an archaeological museum there is every reason *not* to completely gap-fill a broken pot. Similarly, filling the cracks between sherds which have been joined should not be necessary if the joining has been carried out skilfully.

There is also the question of the ultimate destination of the restored pot. If it is to go into store, then full gap-filling is unnecessary and it is only necessary to make the pot strong enough to handle.

In many cases, however, the curator will want gap-filling taken to completion. This is not controversial provided that the original shape is known, as it will be for a wheel-thrown pot. However, the restoration of sculpture must always raise uncertainties when missing fingers, noses, or even whole limbs need to be added. As far as the British Museum is concerned, the final decision lies with the individual curator. The result is that there is no policy for the museum as a whole, so while some departments have removed old restorations from sculpture in recent years, others are having many pieces fully restored.

The existence of old restoration on an object raises the question of whether it should be removed and 'modernised'. Where the object has been wrongly restored, dismantling in the light of further research is normally regarded as essential. However, in many cases, old restorations must be retained because of their historical importance (Vaughan 1992). This may relate to the history of aesthetic appreciation, or it may relate to the history of conservation. In either case, restoration carried out before about 1920[2] must be examined and recorded, and only removed when neither the curator nor the conservator feel that it serves any documentary purpose.

One exception to this rule is where restoration of one object has been carried out with bits of another. This is not a problem with restorations of recent years, but many objects conserved in the nineteenth century were restored in this way, and examples can be drawn from stone, ceramics and metals, and probably from other materials as well. Under normal circumstances they should always be dismantled, although their full documentation is important for the history of conservation.

If gap-filling and making-up are subjects on which opinions are divided, the question of reshaping distorted objects is even more controversial. For some reason, however, the reshaping of organic objects, such as baskets or clothing, does not excite curators and conservators in the way that reshaping metal objects does.

The question of reshaping should revolve around the time and purpose of the distortion. Thus, restoration of damage which occurred at the time of, or since, discovery should be non-controversial (but it sometimes is) while restoration of damage to objects which were deformed before they were lost or abandoned should only be carried out after a careful debate.

A good example of an important object being damaged at the moment it was found was the Coppergate Anglo-Saxon helmet. It was found on a building site in York in 1982 when it was damaged by a mechanical shovel (Tweddle 1992). Few would quibble (though some did) with the decision to restore the original shape, particularly as there was no doubt that the original shape was achieved by the restoration. The helmet had been constructed by rivetting together a number of components made of iron sheet, and some of these were distorted and the rivets sheared at the time of the helmet's discovery. Most of the metal was reshaped without heating in order not to affect the metallographic structure. It was done with specially constructed clamps which were gently screwed up until the correct shape was re-established (McIntyre *et al* 1992). The shape is undoubtedly correct as the original rivet holes were used to hold the pieces of iron together again, although steel bolts were used with heads modified to look like rivets from the outside. Clearly the reshaping process cannot be reversed, but the modern 'rivets' can be removed at will. The strange allegation that 'slight distortions to the helmet were removed making it perfectly symmetrical, removing what must have been part of the helmet's history' (Corfield 1988, 264) is demonstrably untrue, as can be seen from the scale drawings published by Tweddle (1992).

Potentially controversial, however, is the restoration of objects which have been deliberately damaged before burial. The bending or breaking of weapons before placing in a ritual deposit is one instance, as is the deformation of objects which were looted or stolen in antiquity and then buried for safe keeping. An example of the recent reshaping of objects deliberately deformed in antiquity is the conservation of some Roman silver drinking cups known as the Hockwold Treasure (Johns 1986). The thirty-three fragments of silver in the hoard appeared to represent the remains of at least five silver cups, but there was a problem; there were (apparently) thirteen handles, not the expected ten. In their crushed condition, it was impossible to reconcile the bowls with the handles and pedestal feet, so, after debating the issue, it was decided to restore the cups (Oddy and Holmes 1992). First, however, an electroformed replica was made of one of the bowls and what appeared to be the associated handles and foot.

The principal argument *against* restoration is that the bowls were deliberately damaged before burial. The principal argument *for* restoration is that Roman silver cups are very rare and much art historical and technical information would be gained by restoration. In fact, restoration showed that only *four* complete cups were present in the hoard, together with a pedestal foot from a fifth and handles from a sixth and seventh.

What makes this restoration acceptable to many people is that photographs of the fragments as found have been published and the restored cups are important examples of Roman tableware. However, it must be admitted that not everyone will agree with the restoration of deliberately deformed objects.

Between the instances of objects damaged *before* burial or loss and those damaged *at the time* of recovery are those objects which have been damaged *during* burial, for instance by the collapse of a burial chamber. A classic example is the Sutton Hoo treasure which contained many pieces of Byzantine silver.

Only one piece has been reshaped, the so-called Anastasius dish, and no one could now approve of the flame annealing which was carried out in the 1940s before the dish had been properly examined scientifically. Other pieces, such as the fluted bowl, remain in their crushed condition which demonstrates the force of the burial chamber collapse. Indeed, the fluted bowl smashed into a small ladle causing the bowl of the ladle to be damaged by the footring of the dish. Whether or not these objects should be restored is a matter for the relevant curator, but they could be, and their present condition has certainly been fully recorded and published (Bruce-Mitford 1983, 1-201).

One other category of objects are those where the origins of the damage are unknown. The recent reshaping of the Bronze-Age Bush Barrow gold lozenge (185mm x157mm) is a case in point (Kinnes *et al*, 1988). By the time it was deposited in the British Museum in 1922, it was already somewhat crumpled with tears to its edges, having been in Devizes Museum since 1878 and before that in a private collection in Wiltshire since its discovery in 1808. However, subsequent handling by generations of students and scholars has certainly not helped its condition.

As a result of a loan request, the British Museum Department of Conservation carried out a conservation treatment in 1985 which consisted of gently smoothing out the worst creases so that the edges of the various tears came together. The result was a slightly domed shape, the originality of which has been disputed (Shell and Robinson 1988).

Those who doubt that the lozenge was originally domed claim that the British Museum stretched the metal when smoothing out the major creases. However, examination of the lozenge in its present condition shows that it is *not* completely smooth and still retains random minor irregularities to the surface. These would not have remained if the metal had been stretched as has been claimed. Another piece of evidence said to cast doubt on the domed shape are detailed measurements made on a 'cast' (*recte* mould) of an electroformed replica made in 1922. These measurements were made with a reproducibility of ±0.003mm (Shell and Robinson 1988)!

However, these measurements were made on a silicone rubber mould, the dimensions of which will be different from those of the electroform because silicone rubber shrinks on setting. The shrinkage will have been at least 0.5% linearly, and possibly more depending on how the mould was made and whether any anti-shrinkage precautions were taken. But if the new mould will have shrunk, the one used to make the original electroform in 1922 will have shrunk even more because moulding materials used in those days were even less dimensionally stable than modern ones. This is, then, a situation where measurements with a reproducibility of ± 0.003mm are being made on an object which has, in effect, shrunk twice by an unknown amount.

The results of these measurements are illustrated by Shell and Robinson (1988, figs. 4a, 4b) and described as showing that 'the surface of the electrotype is close to or essentially flat' (1988, 252). In fact, Shell and Robinson's illustrations (figs. 4a, 4b) demonstrate no such thing. They show a series of undulating traverses. Whether the lozenge was originally either flat or domed is unclear from this evidence as it had already been distorted by 1922.

The distortions are apparent in both the photographs and in the measurements of the mould of the electrotype. However, because of the unknown amount of shrinkage, the absolute magnitude of the lozenge can never be determined in this way.

It is, of course, true that the restoration of the Bush Barrow lozenge is irreversible, but it was carried out by a skilled conservator using non-metallic tools and without applying the sort of pressure that would be necessary to stretch the metal. That the lozenge was domed is incontrovertible, and even the (admittedly dubious) measurements of the sceptics led them to admit this as a possibility.

Once a restoration has been carried out, the question of re-touching or in-painting must often be faced. This is not normally a problem with gold or silver, but it may be with bronze as the processes of reshaping may have damaged the surrounding patina, or altered its colour as a result of local heating. Re-touching is more of a problem with ceramics and fine art, and many solutions have been attempted in order to blend in the restoration without making it invisible.

Again, curators often differ in their requirements, but are usually influenced by the type of object. If it is essentially archaeological, re-touching will blend in but be visible; if it is a piece of fine or decorative art, there will be a real temptation to attempt an invisible restoration.

Finally, 'restoration' may include the making of a so-called conservation mount. This is a cradle to intimately support the object over a large part of the underside. Such cradles are usually moulded to fit the object, and range from a simple shallow tray, for heavily corroded iron sword blades, to a complex three-dimensional cradle made of glass-fibre reinforced polyester, to support the cauldron chain from Sutton Hoo (Bruce Mitford 1983, fig. 364).

This paper has considered what is meant by restoration mainly from the point of view of the conservators and curators of antiquities. But the restoration of computers, clocks, musical instruments, applied art in general, and easel paintings raises a host of other considerations which have been problems in the past and will continue to be debated in the future. In considering the 'acceptability' of restoration, the people whose views are considered are the relevant curators/owners and the conservator's professional colleagues. But what about the public? And what is the answer if the public demand a different result from that required by the curator and by the conservation profession? In fact, has anyone ever consulted the public about what they expect from the 'restorer', and would any notice be taken if they were consulted?

The final message of this paper is that all possible audiences must be consulted about the end result of restoration, and if, as I suspect, public expectation differs from professional objectives, we, as conservators, need to mount a PR campaign to explain to the public what it is we seek to achieve, and why.

The following papers are one step in the direction of this explanation.

NOTES

1. Third edition, revised and corrected, Oxford 1977

2. 1920 is a purely arbitrary date, but coincides with the introduction of scientific methods of conservation in the British Museum. Other dates could be suggested, such as the time at which full conservation documentation began in any particular institution.

REFERENCES

Bruce-Mitford, R. 1983. *The Sutton Hoo Ship Burial*. Vol. 3 (2 vols.) (ed. A.C. Evans), London

Corfield, M. 1988. The Reshaping of Archaeological Metal Objects: some Ethical Considerations. *Antiquity* **62** (235), 261-5

Johns, C. 1986. The Roman Silver Cups from Hockwold, Norfolk. *Archaeologia* **108**, 137-50

Kinnes, I.A., Longworth, I.H., McIntyre, I.M., Needham, S.P., and Oddy, W.A., 1988. Bush Barrow Gold. *Antiquity* **62** (234), 24-39

McIntyre, I.M., Newey, H.M. and Oddy, W.A. 1993. Reconstruction. in D. Tweddle 1992, *op.cit.* 936-40

Oddy, A. and Holmes, R. 1992. The Hockwold Treasure. in *The Art of the Conservator* (ed. A. Oddy), 137-50. London

Shell, C.A. and Robinson, P. 1988. The recent Reconstruction of the Bush Barrow Lozenge Plate. *Antiquity* **62** (235), 248-60

Smith, S. 1992. The Portland Vase. in *The Art of the Conservator*. (ed. A. Oddy), 42-58. London

Tweddle, D. 1992. *The Anglian Helmet from Coppergate*. (2 vols.) The York Archaeological Trust and the Council for British Archaeology, London

UKIC 1983. *Guidance for Conservation Practice*.

Vaughan, G. 1992. The restoration of Classical Sculpture in the Eighteenth Century and the Problem of Authenticity. in *Why Fakes Matter*, (ed. M. Jones), 41-50. London

Williams, N. 1989. *The Breaking and Remaking of the Portland Vase*. London

RESTORING WHAT WASN'T THERE: RECONSIDERATION OF THE EIGHTEENTH-CENTURY RESTORATIONS TO THE LANSDOWNE *HERAKLES* IN THE COLLECTION OF THE J PAUL GETTY MUSEUM

Jerry Podany

The J Paul Getty Museum, Malibu, California 90265-5799

INTRODUCTION

The title of this conference *Restoration - Is It Acceptable?* asks a question that is deceivingly simple. There are innumerable definitions for the word 'acceptable' and an even greater variety of circumstances under which any of them may appear contradictory. Even the term 'restoration', carrying as it does a rather negative connotation in modern times, is considerably broader in its practical definition than is conventionally recognised. Yet even ignoring these more semantic aspects of the question, it must be recognised that conservators and curators alike spend enormous amounts of time grappling with the complexities of reintegration, completion, cleaning, and presentation. Difficult questions are continually raised, such as: 'Should conservators, scientists and curators attempt to reinstate *all* or even *some* aspects of an artefact's original form?' Indeed, even if the answer is 'Yes', it must be asked if such an achievement can actually be realised. The conservation profession as a whole has turned for assistance in this dilemma to rather broadly stated ethical codes and guidelines, such as the Venice charter of 1964. Such documents encourage the clear delineation of what is original and what is restored. But the ultimate vagueness of these guidelines often results in variable applications of the philosophy. Their viability may depend as much upon the material characteristics or age of an object as it might on the object's relative importance. But whether restoration is 'acceptable' is not the issue to be explored in this paper. The aim is rather to use a specific object in the collections of the Getty Museum to explore whether or not *de-restoration* is acceptable. And if it is, at what costs to the history of the object. It has been reported that in discussing the fate of a number of important ancient sculptures and monuments, a scholar once noted that both a tragedy and a disaster had befallen the Aegina relief housed in Munich in this last century. The tragedy was the damage it suffered in World War II and the disaster, by this scholar's standards, was the later removal of the Thorvaldsen restorations (Ettlinger 1975).

While the comparison in this statement is surely extreme, since it is widely accepted that many of the interpretations carried out by Thorvaldsen were incorrect, the statement serves as a reminder that many of the recent de-restorations intended to free sculpture from 'polluting' restorations have not always gone unchallenged. While the philosophical tenets which guide these de-restorations appear quite unassailable, they may in some cases obscure and even ignore the historical value of what was removed. The desire to uncover and exhibit only the 'honest' and 'pure' core of the ancient form has fuelled many of these removals and there has been little regard for the visual impact of the revealed scars imposed by the earlier restoration techniques. Equally often what was removed has been replaced by modern 'purist' or 'objective' fills and completions. Distinct in their modernity, these forms intentionally present a clearly twentieth-century monochromatic and foreign surface, presuming as a result, an unattached perfection and objectivity. But such presumptions ignore the effect of yet another anachronistic layer added to an already irretrievably altered antiquity.

This paper does not take the position that making clear distinctions between ancient material and modern additions is incorrect. Quite the contrary, what is sought in these discussions is a re-evaluation of the value placed on earlier restorations; a reconsideration of the assumption that their removal is correct; and an examination of the motivations for, and visual impact of, replacing these earlier restorations with yet another style of visual and ethical philosophy.

Seymour Howard in his book *Antiquity Restored: Essays on the After Life of the Antique*, (Howard 1990) notes that the restoration process is like the associative reactions to Rorschach blots, '... images into which the perceiver projects his fantasy, intelligence, faith, understanding, desires, expectations, intent, meaning, preoccupations, etc., thereby revealing as much or more of himself and his world as of the object of contemplation'. Howard later goes on to sum up his observations by saying that 'restoration reflects the postures and rhetoric of the time [it is carried out]'.

It was these and many other comments of scholars and historians which led to a reconsideration of the early restorations of a life-size marble sculpture of Herakles in the Getty collection. A very important part of that reconsideration was the inevitable questioning of the actions taken in the late 1970s to remove these early restorations. A retrospective view of the appearance of the sculpture after its late 1970s restoration presented a mixed and severely anachronistic visual character, one which spoke no less clearly (or loudly) about eighteenth-century restoration techniques or twentieth-century conservation ethics than about the object's original form and ancient appearance.

BACKGROUND

In 1976 the Lansdowne *Herakles* (named in reference to Lord Lansdowne whose collection it once graced) was removed from exhibition for treatment. The iron dowels which held in place the previous marble restorations, dating to the late eighteenth century, were reportedly corroding and endangering the ancient marble segments. After complete disassembly of the fragments, both the curator and conservator of the collection at the time decided not to reattach the early restorations but rather to replace a selected number with modern epoxy versions and leave off the remaining restorations altogether. The style of these new restorations promoted stark and dispassionate objectivity as reflected by the choice of materials and the clear delineation between the ancient marble and modern in-filling or part by the manipulation of volume, colour, texture and translucency (Plates 1, 2). The intent was to release the ancient artefact from any interpretation or visual intervention which might interfere with the viewer's perception of the ancient form. Over the eighteen-year period since that most recent restoration the materials did not prove to be as technically suitable as had been hoped, and the approach became increasingly dissatisfying from a visual and aesthetic point of view. The epoxy began to discolour and the edges of the joins showed staining due to adhesive spills and residues from protective masking. Aesthetically the sculpture presented a rather disjointed vision of three distinct era of restoration/conservation philosophy: the ancient surface and form; the gashes, reworking and undulating cuts left by the eighteenth-century restoration techniques; and the modern recessed perfection of the twentieth-century synthetic segments (Plate 3). The sculpture presented an encyclopedic review of restoration philosophies rather than the remains of a Roman work of art.

Additionally there was a growing body of evidence that the sculpture had in fact been more severely recut than previously assumed and that weathering was quite severe, which led to the inevitable question of just how pure the ancient core of the sculpture was, or could be.

All of this encouraged the museum to reconsider the results of the 1970s work. After lengthy discussions the decision was made to once again reattach the earlier restorations, which fortunately had been saved. Amid other reasons for this decision stood the desire to present a unified and clear representation of the sculpture from at least one of its many incarnations. It was also felt that the restorations were very much an intimate part of the sculpture's history, representing as they did a specific interpretation and attitude toward ancient works of art. As such they not only were more visually sympathetic to the ancient fragments, but were of significant historical importance.

In the process of reaching this decision the department of antiquities conservation and the antiquities curators discussed and debated the issues which shaped the earlier actions of both the eighteenth-century restorers and the twentieth-century conservators, as well as the issues and beliefs which influenced the actions the museum was about to undertake. A general review of those issues is presented in this paper.

BRIEF HISTORY OF THE SCULPTURE

The Lansdowne *Herakles* is thought to be a Roman sculpture copied or based upon an original work by the sculptor, Skopas, who produced some of the most admirable sculpture of the fourth century BC.

The figure was reported to have been found near Hadrian's Villa at Tivoli, presumably by Conte Giuseppe Fede, on land owned by the Marefoschi family. It was purchased by Thomas Jenkins in Rome and sold in 1792 to Lord Lansdowne (Lord Shelburne) in London. For over a century and a half, the sculpture stood in a prominent place as one of the three over-life-size Roman sculptures in the collection (Plate 4). Following the death of Lord Lansdowne, Lord Wycombe took possession of the marbles in 1805. However in 1810 they again were sold to the 3rd. Marquess of Lansdowne (Howard 1978). The *Herakles* was then brought to auction in March 1930 in a Christies sale and entered the collection of J Paul Getty in 1951 as one of the first antiquities John Paul Getty purchased.

EIGHTEENTH-CENTURY RESTORATIONS OF THE *HERAKLES*

One of the earliest reference we have to the condition of the *Herakles* is an 1809 print by J. Agar in *Specimens of Ancient Sculpture in Great Britain*, plate 40 (Plate 5). It confirms in part Seymour Howard's observations, which were contained in a 1954 report to the Getty Museum, that the statue was quite heavily restored. Among the areas that he noted as most prominently reworked, were the forehead and both thighs. Indeed a close inspection of the head reveals extensive recutting of the brow and a typical texturing of the recut area to 'harmonise' the newly smoothed surface with the more weathered area (Plate 6). This action suggests that the surface of the object may in fact not have been as extensively repolished as once assumed (Howard 1978, conservator's report). Howard noted that in general the quality of the restoration was rather poor. This led him to believe that it could not have been done by the master restorer and sculptor Bartolomeo Cavaceppi. Cavaceppi was one of the greatest restorers known during the eighteenth century and a master at the craft of inventive deception. However in 1790, when the Herakles was uncovered, Cavaceppi would have been 74. While it remains possible that he carried out this work at his advanced age, it is more likely that one of his students, already well known for their restoration abilities, would have been contracted under Cavaceppi's influence. Candidates for such a task would have included Carlo Albacini or Giovanni Pierantoni. The former is most likely, since Carlo Albacini (1716-1799) had risen to considerable fame as a restorer by the late-eighteenth century, completing such commissions as the Townley *Discobolos* and the restoration of the Farnese collection for the court of Naples (Vaughan 1991). By the 1770s Albacini had, in fact, already eclipsed his instructor and was viewed in greater favour by the British collectors. He had also won the admiration of many powerful sponsors such as Goethe and Canova. Nonetheless, Albacini, like many of the other restorers of the time, would not have been fully independent of Cavaceppi's influence, since Bartolomeo Cavaceppi had established, for all intents and purposes, the practice of restoration as a considered and admirable activity, raising it above its previously lowly position. He had set the standards for techniques and guided the way to more restrained interpretations which showed a more historical approach to restoration than did the earlier, more freely inventive, Baroque style of restoration.

THE MODERN DE-RESTORATION AND RESTORATION

In 1976 it was reported that the iron pins holding both the restorations and the ancient fragments in place were showing signs of significant corrosion. As a result, iron stains were observed near the joins and there was a fear that the marble would begin to fracture and split. Fracturing was already observed in the upper right arm and it was thought that this was due to the increased volume of the corroded iron. A decision was made to carry out extensive conservation treatment. All segments of the sculpture which had previously been rejoined or restored were disassembled. The iron pins and the lead which held them in place were removed.

Having all the various fragments of the sculpture now disassembled, the curator and conservator of antiquities decided not to reassemble the sculpture but rather to leave aside all of the eighteenth-century restorations. Only those restorations which were necessary for physical support or for 'aesthetic reasons' (Howard 1978, conservators report) were to be replaced. Replacement, however, was carried out using synthetic forms rather than the earlier marble segments.

The major marble restoration segments which were set aside and not replaced included:
- a large back part of the lion skin;
- tip of the nose;
- both extremities of the club;
- the right thumb;
- tip of the left thumb;
- most of the little finger;
- the second joint of the left index finger.

The marble restorations which were set aside but replaced by modern segments were:
- the right forearm and wrist;
- a large chip from the right thigh;
- the whole left calf;
- small chips in the left wrist;
- the area above the right, rear elbow;
- the area behind the right knee;
- the centre of the left arm including the elbow.

The segments were replaced in order to 'hide technical joins' which, it is assumed, were meant to bridge the large gaps between ancient parts in a more suitable and less distracting manner than simply leaving an exposed stainless steel supporting pin. The new segments which served as these aesthetic bridges were made of a thin Pliacre (thixotropic epoxy paste) shell filled with polyurethane foam. In some areas the epoxy paste shells were reinforced with fibreglass cloth. These additions were modelled very closely after the previous marble restorations, however, their surfaces were worked to a smooth perfection and made slightly recessed from the original marble. Additionally these new segments were opaque and monochromatic adding to the clear delineation between the ancient fragments and the modern additions.

A new stainless steel rod, fitted to the back of the sculpture, provided the major anchor and support once the object was placed upon a new pedestal. In the eighteenth-century restoration, an iron rod was embedded in a channel cut deeply into the right leg and thigh and partially hidden by an addition of marble drapery. The new support rod stood quite separate from the sculpture (approximately 12cm from the figure itself) and only utilised the upper end of the channel to anchor into the sculpture proper. The channel was filled with epoxy paste to minimise its visual impact. The marble base, which was reported to be of eighteenth-century manufacture, and which surrounded the ancient foot plinth, was removed and unfortunately was not retained.

RECONSIDERATION

Until the 1976 restoration the *Herakles* stood as a representative example of the eighteenth-century restorer's approach to restoration, both technically and aesthetically (Plate 1). After 1976 the sculpture represented a more 'modern' view (Plate 2), one which is coloured by the late nineteenth-century and twentieth-century romance with materials and 'honesty' as derived from those materials. We note that the conservator's explanation for the removal of the eighteenth-century restorations and defense of the modern additions was: 'The new restoration of the statue was not only made for technical reasons, but also to show the original as much as possible free of alien additions. The emphasis is now on what is left of the original, with additions limited to those necessary to cover the technical joins.' (Howard 1978, conservators report.) Clearly an assumption was made that the modern and intense respect for ancient surfaces and the disdain for past restoration approaches would guide actions that could only assist in a better understanding of the object. However, consideration of the value of the previous work, as well as the impact of removing this work seemed less considered. Two approaches and philosophies representing two distinct era and views of antiquity were at odds. To better understand the conflict between these two approaches, their intentions and their results, it is paramount to explore each further.

EARLY RESTORATIONS

From the mid 1700s to the late 1800s a series of enormous, progressive advances took place in many of the fields which directly or indirectly came to shape our modern view of restoration. Beyond what the French artists and sculptors of the Roman Baroque, such as Bernini, Girardon and Monnot, brought to the restorers, chemistry and art history (as well as the burgeoning discipline of art theory) were making new discoveries and pronouncements. In science there began an investigation of colour and colour perception, such as Newton's *Optiks*, which Barbara Whitney Keyser (1990) recognises as one of the key influences in her discussion of the history of conservation and museology. Such efforts influenced, if not began, the progress of the arts towards a colour theory. At around the same time the German scholar Johann Joachim Winkelman began to systemise the study of antiquity and its material culture. Restorers, close to both by necessity and interested in both by design, began to consider a more scientific and orderly approach to their work. The concept of 'historical accuracy' was now one of their tools and an additional responsibility. Under this influence Antonio Canova, for example, refused to restore the figures by Phidias that Lord Elgin had brought from the Parthenon to London, saying it would be a sacrilege to touch them (Jokileto 1985). Nonetheless, during those years before the early nineteenth century, many parts of the Mediterranean, especially the areas around Rome, were regularly 'mined' for sculpture to satisfy the growing needs of the Grand Tour enthusiasts But *broken* was not *beautiful* and certainly not *marketable*. However, even in this frenzy of enthusiastic appreciation and almost rampant excavation, there was a growing reconsideration of the value of unassaulted antiquity. Such a value had already begun to be recognised in the early-sixteenth century in the High Renaissance. Unlike earlier restorations, which permitted a great deal of invention and free interaction born of the earlier *imitatio* and the *all'antica* style (Gombrich 1963), the late eighteenth-century approach was far more empathetic to the neoclassical forms themselves. Though viewers may be off-put by the extent to which the restorer intervened, it must be said that restraint of hand was greater than perhaps at any other time in the previous history of restoration. Quickly fading was the extensive and fanciful enlargement of single fragments beyond any vague reference to the original objects, leading to such extensive pastiches that they might be better termed fakes.

Nonetheless, objects were seldom sold unless restored and that restoration rarely, if ever, even approached our modern sensibilities of complete respect for the ancient surface and form. The completion of a sculpture depended upon an interpretive approach and, irrespective of the increasingly historical basis for this interpretation, it was nonetheless based more on aesthetic opinion and desire than on fact. By the time Albacini came to command a high position in the world of British collectors and European dealers, fragments were increasingly salvaged for their own sake and caution was entering the vocabulary of many sculpture restorers. Such a progression led to our modern sensibilities and many of the finer examples of early restoration activity should stand as historic documents, providing, as they do, a window into the history of a period, and also a window to our modern views.

THE MODERN APPROACH

The clear intention of the 1970s restoration was to remove 'pollution', assuming as it did that the earlier restorations were misleading and dishonest, and that they somehow concealed the beauty and intent of the ancient fragments. Indeed cases abound in which restoration, carried out with free interpretive license, obscured and reinvented the original form of the sculpture. E. Van de Wetering once noted that after seeing the Myron *Discobolos* without its additions he realised that the sculpture presented an entirely different approach to sculpting the human form (Wetering 1979). The anatomical detail of the additions and their clear dependence on a sub-structure below the surface, carried this approach throughout the object. Free from these additions, however, the sculpture revealed a pre-Michelangelo 'limitation' to the surface, a much more abstract treatment of the form. But Van de Wetering does not discuss the effect of the cleanly cut, undulating joint surfaces which were carved to accept the restoration fittings and were, as a result of de-restoration, exposed. These surface scars, which spoke of a once hidden process and not of sculptural form, have no relationship to the outer volume of the sculpture itself and as such assault the eye as foreign and interruptive. They speak of repaired damage and of intervention, irreversible and lasting. Perhaps Van de Wetering looked beyond these scars and accepted them as unfortunate tragedies in the war of philosophical precepts. In his ability to limit his sight he presents, however, the focal confines of a twentieth-century interpreter. Willing to accept as unfortunate these scars of past restorations, but not as part of the object's history, he is also willing to accept the loss of another period's interpretation, preferring his own time's understanding and definition of 'truth'.

The 'truth' of ancient fragments is, by our modern guidelines, best understood with, at most, absolute minimal intervention of our own time. This is taken to mean both physical and visual intervention. The conflict of this restraint on intervention with the desire, if not the need to, complete or unify a fragmented form, by applying an almost purely *Gestaltist* approach to the treatment of integrative additions has been addressed. The *Gestalt* claim, woven in assumptions that the human mechanism of perception relegates *insignificant* stimuli to the viewer's perceptual background, was ready-made for the twentieth-century conservator's desire to *remain objective when it came to interpretation*. Like the many black and white, two dimensional forms which the *Gestalt* used to examine the visual foregrounds and backgrounds of our perceptive processes, the conservator assumed that a neutrally toned, undecorated, untextured field would be relegated to the visual background and still complete its purpose of providing unity among separated fragments. If the additions were painted a 'neutral colour' and recessed' from the original volume they would be perceptually recessed and visually neutral. The 'rules' of perception would be clear should the viewer break out of the assumed constraints of the visual structure. What was smooth and monochromatic was modern and what was rough and weathered was ancient. A discussion of whether we have been successful, or even involved, in sufficiently communicating these rules is not within the realm of this paper. What is clear, however, is that the viewer of sculpture, either of historical artefact or expressive work of art, does not set his or her perception to work the same way as might be done with a bichromatic flat shape. The surface of a sculpture is scoured for meaning, subtle form and hidden relief. Unified motion, dimensional shifts and volumetric expression is relished. In such an active relationship with the object before us, very little is actually relegated to a perceptual background, since very little is considered 'insignificant'. As a result, these forms of objective perfection become contestants, vying for the attention of the viewer and, in some cases, emerging from the visual struggle victorious. At times the total effect is one of chaos, an anachronistic collection of assembly philosophies and not a unified vision of what was assembled.

While the approach described here can indeed be applied quite successfully and in some instances is the only answer which can be applied if respect for the original fragment is to be maintained, there is a great deal to be gained by evaluating its wholesale application to all sculptural works. More germane to this paper, there is a great deal to be gained by reconsidering the assumption that this 'purist' approach will be an improvement (or even more 'pure') than those taken by previous generations of restorers. The value of the ancient form cannot be disputed, but the influence of any additions, irrespective of their philosophical grounds and visual context to that ancient forms, must not be ignored.

CONCLUSIONS

As stated in the beginning of this paper the effort of this reconsideration has not been to deny the advancements made in the modern professions of conservation and curatorial studies. These advancements have resulted in a full respect for ancient surfaces and fragmentary forms. Nor has this paper been put forward to argue with the clear and needed delineation of modern reintegration and restoration with the original material. All of these advancements and tenets have kept the interpretive hand at bay, and the evidence which the artefact brings to this and future generations of scholars remains clear and unaltered. But neither does this reconsideration conclude that there is no value in past restorations nor that our modern sensibilities do not effect the future perception of ancient works. What has been discussed encourages a careful consideration of what earlier restorations contribute to our view of antiquities. It also cautions that most actions by earlier restorers are, to all intents and purposes, permanent and irreversible. What is retrievable by de-restoration may be less valuable to the study of antiquity than the earlier restoration was to the study of a more recent century.

REFERENCES

Arnheim, R. 1954. *Art and Visual Perception*. Berkeley, California

Bober, P.P. and Rubenstein, R. 1986. *Renaissance Artists and Antique Sculpture*. London

Brandi, C. 1963. *Teoria del Restauro*. Rome

Brandi, C. 1963. Il Trattamento Delle Lacune E La Gestalt Psycologie. in *Problems of the 19th and 20th Centuries: Studies in Western Art* (Acts of the Twentieth International Congress of the History of Art, Vol.IV), 146-51. Princeton

Ceschi, C. 1970. *Teoria e Storia del Restauro*. Rome

Coremans, P. 1963. Discussion reported in *Problems of the 19th and 20th Centuries: Studies in Western Art* (Acts of the Twentieth International Congress of the History of Art, Vol.IV), 167. Princeton

Ettlinger, L.D. 1975. From a speech at the opening of an exhibition at the Akademisches Kunst Museum in Bonn, devoted to the elements of the Aeginetan *Warriors* made by Thorvaldsen. Pers. comm. Dr. Salvatore Settis

Feilden, B. 1979. The Unification of the Principles of Restoration. in *Problems of the Completion of Art Objects* (Proceedings of the Second International Restorers Seminar), 19-34. Vészprem, Hungary

Gombrich, E.H. 1963. The Style All'Antica: Imitation and Assimilation. in *The Renaissance and Mannerism: Studies in Western Art* (Acts of the Twentieth International Congress of the History of Art, Vol.II), 31-41. Princeton

Haskell, F. and Penny, N. 1981. *The Taste and the Antique.* London

Howard, S. 1970. Bartolomeo Cavaceppi and the Origins of Neo Classic Sculpture. *The Art Quarterly*, **XXXIII** (2), 120-33

Howard, S. 1990. *Antiquity Restored: Essays on the Afterlife of the Antique.* IRSA, Vienna

Howard, S. 1978. *The Lansdowne Herakles.* J Paul Getty Museum, Malibu

Jokelito, J. 1985. Authenticity in Restoration Principles and Practices. *APT* **XVII** (3 and 4), 5-11

Jurgen, P. 1972. Antikenerganzung und Ent-Restaurierung. *Kunst-Chronik*, April 1972, 85-112

Keyser, B.W. 1990. History of Conservation and the Teaching of Museology. in Preprints *ICOM Committee for Conservation: 9th Triennial Meeting, Dresden, GDR, 26-31.8.90*, Vol.1, 373-83

Lattimore, S. 1975. Two Statues of Herakles. *J Paul Getty Museum Journal*, **2**, 17-26

Lelekov, L.A. 1981. Theoretical Aspects of Restoration. in *ICOM Committee for Conservation: 6th Triennial Meeting, Ottawa, 1981*, 81/11/5-1 to 5-7

Smith, R.D. 1988. Reversibility: A questionable Philosophy. *Restaurator*, 9 (1), 199-207

Vaughan, G. 1991. Albacini and his English patrons. *Journal of the History of Collections*, **3** (2), 183-98

Welford, A.T. 1970. Perceptual Selection and Integration. *Ergonomics* **13** (1), 5-23

Wetering, E. Van De, 1979. Theoretical Considerations With Respect To The Completion Of Works Of Art. in *Problems of the Completion of Art Objects* (Proceedings of the Second International Restorers Seminar), 47-57, Vészprem, Hungary

Yakhont, O.V. 1990. Methods Aspects of Restoration Completions. in Preprints *ICOM Committee for Conservation: 9th Triennial Meeting, Dresden, GDR, 26-31.8.90*, Vol 1, 396-8

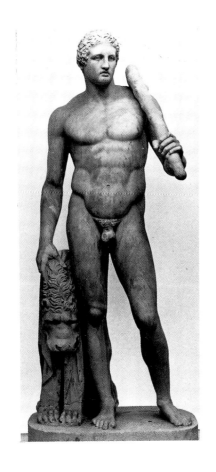

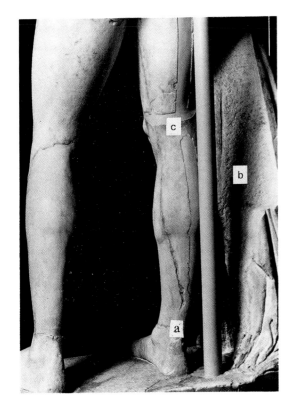

Plate 1 (above left)
The Lansdowne *Herakles* with the late eighteenth-century restorations still in place

Plate 2 (above right)
The eighteenth-century restorations removed and the synthetic fills and completions of the late 1970s installed

Plate 3 (left)
One view of the sculpture after the 1970s treatment, which shows three distinct 'periods' of the sculpture's history presented at once: a. the ancient surface; b. remnants of the late eighteenth-century restoration; and c. the twentieth-century synthetic fills and completions

17

Plate 4   A view of the gallery in the Lansdowne mansion which exhibited the *Herakles*
(from S. Howard *The Lansdowne Herakles* The J. Paul Getty Museum, 1978 Malibu)

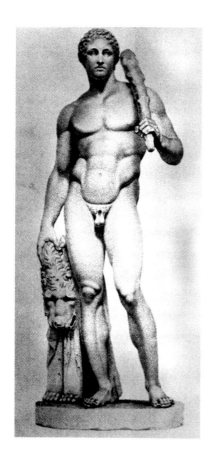

Plate 5   An 1809 drawing of the Herakles
Plate 6   Stippling of the recut surface on the ancient section of the head as well as on the restoration
segment to harmonise the textures

OBJECTS AS SYSTEMS:
A NEW CHALLENGE FOR CONSERVATION[1]

Suzanne Keene

The Science Museum, Exhibition Road, South Kensington, London SW7 2DD

The objective of this paper is to examine the thinking that has been taking place on conserving computer systems from the perspective of 'conventional' conservation ethics and professional practice, and to see if useful parallels can be drawn with approaches to the conservation and use of other types of object.

CONSERVATION ETHICS

At the foundation of the conservation ethic lies the precept 'thou shalt not change the nature of the object' (UKIC 1981). Ethics are necessary in conservation because the processes which take place can drastically alter the object. It is not possible to specify and supervise such complex work in sufficient detail for total control: therefore it is necessary to indoctrinate the practitioners with general values which will determine, or at least influence, how they act. Once people have been inculcated with a value system, they cannot be expected to violate it to order. You would not, for example, be able to find a surgeon in the U.K. who would amputate your leg if there was nothing wrong with it; medical ethics would preclude it.

In the precepts generally adopted in conservation ethics, conservation is seen as the perpetuation of the object-as-evidence about past technology, values, or use. Alterations to the object are more and more being kept to a minimum. This is in order that museums can meet their obligations to maintain collections as the basis for study and research, and to show users and visitors, as far as possible, 'the real thing': objects from which they can draw their own conclusions, rather than objects altered to conform to a particular viewpoint or passing taste (Swade 1993). Minimising conservation is also an acknowledgement that conservation treatments have often failed in the past, and that many heavily altered objects have been devalued because of changes in taste or display fashion.

THE ROLES OF OBJECTS IN MUSEUMS

MacDonald and Alsford (1991) discuss the foundation for preserving the object-as-evidence from the museological point of view. They point out that the importance of original objects is now being challenged by, for example, science centres, children's museums, and ecomuseums in which the emphasis is on demonstrating the processes of science rather than objects. They go on to argue that, on the other hand, the fundamental product of museums is information: 'Museums are (at the most fundamental level) concerned with information ... and ultimately the wisdom acquired from extensive and experience-enriched knowledge.' ... 'preservation of heritage objects is not an end in itself, but serves to maximise (over time) the access to the information encoded in them.'

Objects in museums, then, are sources of information and of evidence (ideally, primary evidence in the historian's sense), but they are also vehicles for conveying it. Because display or demonstration often affects the value of the object-as-evidence, these functions are sometimes mutually incompatible. In striking a balance, we should bear in mind that conveying information is usually a short-term requirement (indeed, the duration may be self-limiting if the object wears out), whereas maintaining the evidential value of the object keeps options open and serves the museum in the long term. But in science and technology museums the point of the object is often what it does, or did (Mann 1989). Still, we should show 'how this machine was used by people to make widgets in 1888 ...', not 'how we have made this machine make much better widgets than it used to'.

CONSERVATION AND DEMONSTRATION

In 'conventional' museum conservation, efforts are made to restrict work on objects to:

- what is needed to remove or counter factors causing deterioration, plus the minimum work necessary to repair past damage;
- making new parts or adding material if needed to hold the object together or to make it mechanically stable;
- necessary additions to make the object understandable.

All work is documented in order to preserve the evidential value of the object as far as possible. New work is clearly identified but not necessarily obvious. Old parts are only replaced if they constitute a danger to the object. Even then, the original part would be kept as part of the object-as-evidence.

THE CASE AGAINST RUNNING MUSEUM OBJECTS

The implications of running objects have been interestingly explored by Mann (1989, 1990). The conservator's objection to running an object will be that this compromises it as primary evidence. Conservators are usually the people called on to do the work to make objects functional: the objective itself of the work thus conflicts with the values by which their actions are normally determined. Returning an object to operational order will often mean that work with more profound effects has to be carried out on the object than would be the case if it were preserved without running it. Also, the work has to be done in the knowledge that the aim is then to do something with the object that will endanger it as a true record of the past.

Thus apparently incontrovertible ethics are in practice compromised all the time. For example, displaying pictures is closely analogous to running an object, because light causes colour changes, yet dozens of conservators prepare pictures for display in the course of their normal work.

CONSERVING COMPUTERS

Computer conservation has until very recently been undertaken by highly skilled computer engineers and technicians, working with curators, rather than by people with specific conservation training (Swade 1990). There is a difference in approach, partly of course a matter of skills and knowledge. Computer engineers can restore the function of the object: conservators are more knowledgeable about the chemistry of deterioration and how to remedy or prevent this. To a great extent, the knowledge of each is a closed book to the other. A third dimension is the way in which the objective of the exercise is understood and interpreted (the application of conservation ethics), and this can be represented by the curator or by the conservator. What we really need are electronics conservators, knowledgeable about electronics, chemistry and conservation, and ethics.

To preserve a computer, possible conservation measures fall into three main categories (Kingsley 1994; Moncrieff 1994):

1. preservation actions, e.g. removing oil and grime that is likely to promote corrosion and breakdown of plastic insulation, providing mechanical support or joining loose parts, removing components (such as batteries) that have the potential to damage the main object, for separate storage;
2. remedial and pro-active measures, for example, applying antioxidant to insulation;
3. restoration actions, such as replacing wiring in part or in whole, resoldering, replacing blown valves; in general, replacing original parts with new ones.

Replacing 'consumable' parts or parts with a known short lifetime, e.g. valves, can only be somewhat ethically dubious for a museum, as it uses up the finite historic stock of such objects. Can original, historic parts be excluded from the conservation ethic? At least, the original part that came with the object should be kept and clearly identified. The alternative would be to replace the dysfunctional part with a modern component, as often happens with other sorts of working object.

RUNNING COMPUTERS

What are the implications of running computers themselves? Especially in older and large computers, the act of collecting them itself may well have entailed traumatic intervention: for instance, cutting through all the main cables. But returning a computer to working condition will sometimes entail replacing parts or components, or in extreme cases resoldering and rewiring it.

Unlike mechanical objects, electronic components do not wear out, although most computers also have mechanical parts which do wear out - disk drives, keyboards, etc. However, not running such machines may itself be detrimental to them; after a period of inaction they often will not function when switched on. This may simply be because of deterioration over time, or it may be some effect such as that the heat involved in regular running prevents corrosion films forming. If true, it could be argued that regulated use is part of the conservation process. But when a computer is in operation, heat is generated, and this will certainly hasten the deterioration of synthetic materials such as plastic and rubber.

THE INFORMATION GAIN FROM RUNNING COMPUTERS

There is undoubtedly a large information gain from running computers - probably more than from most mechanical objects (Sale 1994; Burton 1994). This may be because computers are much more complex than most mechanical objects (orders of magnitude more complex). If software is included, a computer could have millions of working parts. The actual operation can neither be deduced nor envisaged by examining the physical non-running object. This may be true also of complex machines.

Information is also gained because information in documentation and manuals is often incomplete. It is not unusual for the culminating developments of a technology not to be fully documented. If surviving expertise can be used in the resurrection process, the information on how the machine is maintained and operated can be made more complete, provided that the work is properly captured and documented, using video, photographs, records, etc. The existence of the 'virtual object' part of other objects (i.e. software) may depend on the computer running, if it is the only one available, and no software emulation of it exists.

As with other working objects, once the operational characteristics of the original machine can be studied it can, if required, be reproduced as a replica. In the case of computers, this can be in the form of a software emulation, which can more or less exactly represent the operation, and to some extent the nature, of the original on a modern machine.

INFORMATION LOSS

To set against the information gain, there is likely to be a loss if the physical nature of the object is altered. The physical characteristics of computers are an important determinant for their design and for the efficiency of their operation. Many important developments in computer design and technology have come about through changes in the physical nature of their component parts, the superseding of valves by electronic components being a striking instance of this. In turn, the physical operating characteristics and requirements of computers have determined the design of a whole generation of office buildings. Huge amounts of space between floors to accommodate cabling, cooling and ventilation ducting have only been needed since the spread of information technology in the late 1980s, and this feature will be rendered obsolete if the technology of networking by means of radio or other non-physical means of transmission develops sufficiently.

Apart from information on the history of computing technology to be gained from studying the physical evidence of the object itself, the appearance of the object both inside and out has a powerful impact on the viewer. It is absolutely obvious even to the inexpert that Pegasus, for example, is completely different from a modern PC in many fundamental ways - a much greater difference than that between a horse-drawn carriage and a Vauxhall Astra. So the physical characteristics of computers are important to museums.

CONSERVING SOFTWARE

As a museum object, software can be thought of as having 'physical' parts: the box, the disk, etc., and a 'virtual' part which comes into existence when it runs (Swade 1993; Johnstone 1993). The sole function of a computer is to run software, i.e. to cause the software 'virtual' object to exist. In terms of conservation ethics, software conservation is much less problematic than hardware, although it raises many intriguing questions of analogy.

The physical parts of the software (the box, the shrink wrapping, the disks, etc.) will have exactly the same kind of information value as does any other physical object, and will be subject to the same ethical constraints if they are required to be treated or 'used'. Software media (disks, tapes, etc.) are likely to be very difficult to physically preserve in perpetuity, but this is not a problem we need to address here. The code, the 'virtual' object, can be held to be a separable 'object part'. This part is an ideal subject for conservation because (a) it has no physical existence, and (b) it can easily be replicated. *If* the replicas are exact (bit-perfect) then the 'original' embodiment of the code has no more information value than does any subsequent replica. Printing the code out onto a stable physical medium such as acid-free paper could greatly assist its later remedial conservation (see below). This would be equivalent to a highly detailed physical record, such as a hologram, of a physical object. While the written code would not operate, it could be drawn on if the current replica of the actual code was defective and had to be 'treated'.

The conservation treatment of software code will consist of the following:

1. Preventive conservation
  - storing the code on a physical medium selected to be as stable as   possible so as to minimise subsequent copying
  - if necessary, copying the code onto a new medium at intervals before the shelf life of the existing medium is exceeded
  - ensuring that a computer, whether the original or an emulation, exists on which the 'virtual' object can run.

2. Remedial conservation
  - If a copy of the code turns out to have developed a fault (e.g. copying it has not resulted in a perfect replica of the original) then repairing this fault, by replacing the faulty code with code that will run, will constitute conservation. An analogy would be to retype a sentence in a document if it had become garbled during copying. The same procedures should be followed as are used in documenting normal conservation work: the replacement code should be marked as such, preferably by means of code in the programme (REM's, etc.), and the exact work done should be recorded. In fact, the same conservation record forms as are used for physical conservation can probably be employed.
  - If the original code is faulty and has a mistake in it (i.e. it has a bug) then removing or repairing this bug would constitute *restoration*. The great advantage is that copies of software code may be restored without compromising the original, *as long as the original is identified, retained, and preserved unrestored, and the restoration on the restored version is identified as such.*

Therefore, there is no unique ethical problem about conserving software; questions of the instability of the physical medium are no more problematic than for other objects made of non-stable materials and do not affect the preservation of the 'virtual' object. However, Swade (1993) and Johnstone (1993) are quite right to identify the large requirements for people, time, and skills if software and hardware are to be 'conserved'.

PRESERVING SYSTEMS

Museums which collect modern technology will have to come to terms with the systemic nature of objects which include electronic components and programs. Computers and software cannot be treated separately, although each can be identified as a separate type of object. The particular problem is that the sole purpose of the computer or hardware is to run the software; the software cannot meaningfully exist unless the hardware works. This does not only apply to computers, but also to the multitude of machines with electronic components (especially those with built-in hardware and software, for example analytical machines or electron microscopes). To an extent, at least for computer systems, it is possible to treat the two components of the system independently, by creating a software emulation of the original hardware that will enable the program to run on a newer machine. Burton (1994) and Sale (1994) discuss this. However, this solution is so expensive as to be impractical for all but a few very important machines.

CONCLUSIONS

Many types of object are conserved, or restored, in order to subject them to 'use' that will probably be detrimental, including for instance buildings, musical instruments, and paintings. Computers are just another type of object to take their place in this list. Musical instrument historians, curators and musicians have engaged in a very similar debate for some time, and it could be worth studying their codes of practice (Karp 1985; Myers 1985). In these, the older and rarer and less modified the instrument, the less the justification for restoring it in order to use it. If the instrument is brought to working order, then the maximum information should be gained if and when it is played. For example, performances of historic instruments are made available to as many people as possible by making recordings for sale; technical drawings of them are produced so that exact replicas can be made for the historic music business. These guidelines are very similar to those proposed by Mann for historic vehicles (1990). The case for restoring and running an historic computer may be somewhat strengthened by the argument that only by doing so can software 'virtual' objects exist.

The argument for restoring and running a computer is that this enriches the information dimension of it as a museum object. The conflict between archival and demonstration functions may best be resolved by separating the two requirements: one computer is conserved, frozen in time, as physical evidence, while evidence of function is maintained either by restoring a machine to working order or by creating a replica or emulation. Particularly valuable information may be gained if the process of restoration captures the technical skills and knowledge of the original operators. In this event, there is an obligation to permanently record such information, since eventually the object will cease to work. These considerations are common to many types of object. Unique to computers may be that they are components in a system, in that their sole purpose is to run software, which can only be said to exist if it can be run on a computer. In a sense, perhaps the *system* has an equally strong claim to be an object.

NOTE

1. Some papers on the topic of conserving computers and software are collected together in *Collecting and conserving computers*, seminar papers available from the Coordinator, Collections Management Group, Science Museum, London

REFERENCES

Burton, C. 1994. Historic Machine Simulation in Practice. in *Collecting and conserving computers*, papers from a seminar. Science Museum, London

Johnstone, S. 1993. *Software and the Science Museum.* Science Museum internal report

Karp, C. 1985. Musical Instruments in Museums. *The International Journal of Museum Management and Curatorship*, **4**, 179-82

Kingsley, H. 1994. How can we tackle Conservation? in *Collecting and Conserving Computers*, papers from a seminar. Science Museum, London

MacDonald, G.F. and Alsford, S. 1991. The Museum as Information Utility. *Museum Management and Curatorship*, **10**, 305-11

Mann, P. 1990. The Implications of using Museum Vehicles. in *The Way Ahead: Papers from the First World Forum of Motor Museums*, held at the National Motor Museum, Beaulieu, 6th-10th November 1989 (ed. D. Zeuner), 22-34. World Forum of Motor Museums, Beaulieu

Mann, P.R. 1989. Working Exhibits and the Destruction of Evidence in the Science Museum. *Journal of Museum Management and Curatorship*, **8**, 369-87

Moncrieff, A. 1994. How can we tackle Conservation: Prevention of Damage. in *Collecting and conserving computers*, papers from a seminar. Science Museum, London

Myers, A. 1985. Conservazione, Restauro e Riuso degli Strumenti Musicali Antichi: per una Carta Europea del Restauro. in papers from *Anno Europea della Musica: Convegno Internazionali di Studi, 16-19 Oct. 1985*. Fondazione Levi, Venice

Sale, A. 1994. The Pegasus Restoration and Simulation Project. in *Collecting and conserving computers*, papers from a seminar. Science Museum, London

Swade, D. 1993. Preserving Information in an Object-centred Culture. *History and Computing*, March 1993, 98-102

Swade, D. 1990. Computer Conservation and Curatorship. *Resurrection*, **1**, 1

UKIC, 1981. *Guidance for Conservation Practice*. UKIC, London

CLOCKS AND WATCHES, A RE-APPRAISAL?

Francis E. Brodie
Museum of London, London Wall, London EC2Y 5HN

INTRODUCTION

Traditionally-trained clock and watch-makers are becoming increasingly aware of horological conservation without realising the fuller implications of its meaning. Indeed, it is possible to see advertisements in horological trade publications for conservation and restoration offered by the same firm. The aim of this paper is to clarify the difference between the two disciplines, indicating that a greater gulf exists than is realised. Clocks and watches may be restored for a number of reasons including a desire to have them running, to replace parts assumed to be missing or incorrect, to increase their value or to improve the appearance of damaged parts.

WORKING OF CLOCKS AND WATCHES

It is not proposed, in this paper, to add a great deal to the discussion already being aired concerning the ethics of running on the grounds of wear and tear, but it is worth pointing out that less elaborate domestic-sized clocks, chronometers and larger timepiece watches are worked almost by default because of their ease of operation. Owners, or keepers of collections, in addition to their staff, feel confident in the running of clocks and watches because they are such familiar objects. Generally reliable, even old clocks and watches may perform to a very high standard of accuracy requiring little input in the way of capital and running costs; they hardly present a safety hazard in the way that perhaps a steam-generating boiler might. The accepted wisdom seems to be that running clocks and watches gives pleasure to visitors of collections, or imparts character to the country house setting. If all fails, there still exists an active repair/restoration trade to which work can be contracted; alternatively, as clockwork technology is perceived as straightforward, any dabbler in the employ of the owner might feel confident at dismantling the movement.

It is against this background that I propose to look at what restoration involves in horology, passing over current horological conservation thinking to suggest future developments. The following descriptions of repair/restoration techniques are superficial and not definitive and will be familiar to practising horologists.

RESTORATION OF CLOCKS AND WATCHES

Mechanical clocks and watches, as the name implies, possess moving components including gear trains, levers, springs, etc., all being subject to sliding friction. As the motive force (e.g. mainspring) is restricted by design considerations, the object will only work if friction (a function of lubrication and the effects of wear) does not exceed a certain value.

Lubrication

Horological lubrication methods can present problems. Oil is normally added to a small reservoir at the time of overhaul and often not replenished until the next overhaul. Both the design and scale of common clock or watch-work hinder re-oiling between overhauls, apart from the objection to adding fresh oil to old, possibly contaminated, lubricant. Therefore, from time to time the mechanism must be dismantled for cleaning, oiling and re-assembly. This will present little problem to the experienced horologist, but there is the ever present danger of damage to the exposed movement.

Dismantling

Dismantling is not without its hazards: screw heads may be broken, enamel dials may crack on removal, whilst the component pieces on the bench can easily be lost or their location in the mechanism forgotten (Gould 1931). It is usual with spring-driven movements to remove the mainspring from its housing (barrel) for cleaning, inspection and relubricating. It is not unknown for the walls of the barrel to fail upon re-insertion of the spring, bursting it open. As springs are difficult to handle at this stage, it is always a temptation to use bare hands, with the risk of fingerprinting and rusting.

Shafts (arbors) carrying gear wheels terminate in small diameter pivots which run in bearings (pivot holes) usually in the plates of the movement. When dismantling or reassembling, such pivots are at risk from breakage (especially in smaller clocks and watches), since the pivots have to be inserted into their respective holes in one operation. Striking and chiming mechanisms require the precise meshing of individual teeth, usually resulting in several attempts at reassembly with a potential risk of damage.

Effects of wear and its repair

After a long period of operation, or following lubrication breakdown, it becomes necessary to compensate for wear if the clock or watch is to continue to work. Parts affected include pivot surfaces, pivot holes, meshing faces of gears, acting faces of the escapement, levers, etc. It is customary to polish pivots, sometimes employing a lathe with the attendant dangers of marking the component when mounted in the chuck, the component flying free if gripped gently, or even breaking off the pivot.

The combination of pivot polishing and pivot hole wear frequently results in excessive play in the bearings, and it is customary to close the holes in the plates by various means, including 'punching-up' (using special punches), or inserting a brass plug and opening a new bearing hole (bushing). The second process requires that the original pivot hole and lubricant reservoir (oil-sink) be opened sufficiently to admit a decent sized plug. It is worth noting that English hand-made watch and chronometer rough movements were originally supplied with pivot holes drilled in the approximate position, subsequently to be plugged, accurately located and opened up when the gear wheels were mounted by the finisher (Griffiths 1992).

The process of bushing allows the restorer to alter very subtly the depth of engagement of meshing gears (re-depthing or uprighting), a critical factor if a clock or (in particular) a watch is to run at all. Re-depthing is quite commonly practised during repair especially if a great deal of wear has occurred in the past, but the author is aware of at least one clock where the original depths were found to be incorrect resulting in the non-running of the clock. This example was recently restored to working order by bushing a proportion of the bearings.

After protracted periods of operation, gear teeth show wear at their meshing zones. Many techniques are available to the restorer to alleviate the problem, ranging from complete replacement of affected components such as gear wheels or arbors, to simpler methods such as repositioning laterally or reversing gear wheels on their arbors. Some of these techniques destroy certain components that may be of use to researchers in dating or authenticating examples. In the case of large public (turret) clocks, worn areas on pinions can be rebuilt by means of welding.

Wear is a problem on acting surfaces of the escapement and levers. Slight wear is polished out and, if necessary, components either bent or repositioned. Steel pads (shoes) may be soft-soldered in place over more extensively worn areas; when wear is severe, rebuilding is carried out by hard-soldering larger pieces in position or by complete replacement of the worn component. Any component which the restorer feels will not perform satisfactorily when the clock or watch is reassembled will be adapted, heat treated (including soldering), or replaced. For example, it is possible to repair some types of breakages of mainsprings, but those springs which have lost their elastic properties will be discarded. Mainsprings, notably French ones, were often signed by the maker and dated. Indiscriminate replacement may deny this information to future researchers.

Cleaning

Cleaning follows repairs and, as horological movements contain brass, ammoniacal solutions are commonly employed to remove tarnish, or fingerprints. Such solutions are widely employed owing to their effectiveness and ease of operation; the author has observed that carefully adjusted and aged solutions will remove all traces of tarnish overnight without appearing to etch surfaces too badly. After immersion in this type of cleaner, components may be rinsed, followed by some form of polishing.

Coloured metal finishes, such as blued steel screws or springs, can be at risk, particularly if rusted. The usual procedure is to repolish, sometimes using a rotating steel brush, followed by re-blueing either by direct heating in air or immersion in proprietary blueing salts. Gilding is frequently reapplied to metal cases.

Other areas of restoration include the resilvering of dials, followed by coating using lacquers frequently based on cellulose nitrate. Painted dials tend to be repainted or, if seriously damaged, stripped and repainted afresh. Enamel dials may be restored using epoxy resins or, where more extensively damaged, replaced altogether.

Restoration to improve

More extensive restoration may occur so that a less valuable type may be converted to one of increased value by judicious modifications and additions. Also since clockwork was expected to work, old examples were sometimes modified in the past as technical developments and fashions dictated. In particular, the escapement and pendulum of domestic clocks were updated and in some cases a pendulum would be added where none previously existed. These days, the fashion is to restore clocks back to their presumed original condition, removing later additions whilst adding whole missing sections or signatures (White 1989).

PRESENT-DAY CONSERVATION

As has already been mentioned, horological conservators are likely to have been trained in traditional clock or watchmaking methods. In many cases a conservator will probably carry out broadly similar treatments as outlined above. Perhaps the concentration of ammonia in cleaning solutions might be reduced or substituted with another chemical. In the desire to avoid ammoniacal solutions, mechanical cleaning methods may be employed, the suitability of which may be open to question. Adhesives may be substituted in those circumstances where heat treatment is thought to be too drastic, without consideration of their long-term properties. The conservator may be a contractor working at a distance from the collection and be under pressure to get clocks working, with the need only for an annual inspection. This places the conservator in a dilemma: should he replace those components not thought to be sufficiently sound, or attempt to retain as much of the original as possible but in a repaired state. Horological conservators may attempt to circumvent this by keeping highly detailed records and carefully returning those parts which have been replaced during overhaul for retention by the owner.

FUTURE NEEDS

In what ways, therefore, should horology conservation be heading? Many of the ideas are established in other fields of conservation, and should not be unfamiliar to general object conservators. Some of the ideas are already current in institutions containing clock and watch collections but in a rather piecemeal manner with, it would seem, little understanding of the underlying reasons for their use.

Working of collections

Conservators should not be afraid of having input at an early stage into the selection of which clocks and watches should be run. The author is aware of the desire of some collection managers to have all the examples fully overhauled in one large project, then decide on which ones to keep running. Where a choice of clocks or watches exists in a collection, careful selection must be a priority consideration and possible deciding factors include:

condition — not only the amount of work needed, but degree of originality;
vulnerability — such things as delicacy of hands, dial, glass shades, robustness of movement;
type — some clocks and watches require daily winding, a few are year-going;
environment
staff demands — will there be time allowed for inspections?

Furthermore, questions should be asked to ascertain the likely benefits visitors might gain by seeing working clocks and watches. In those situations, where the mechanism is hidden from view with only the hands visible, there exists the real possibility of replacing the original movements with a substitute of some sort, either electrical, or mechanical. Indeed, one company, formerly a manufacturer of electric clocks, has recently introduced mechanical movements into its range. Doubtless participants will be familiar with pendulum quartz clocks with swinging dummy pendulums, and such ideas could be adapted. Obviously, care and ingenuity are required for such projects, not least in the storage and documentation of the original movements, whilst it should not be forgotten that the hands and dial are still at risk from winding and setting. Alternatives to substitution include models, replicas, videos, computer graphics, etc. Examples of these can, for example, be seen to good effect at the Gershom Parkington collection at Bury St Edmunds and the Old Royal Observatory at Greenwich. It is evident, however, that many of these solutions are expensive and, despite such alternatives, spectacular originals or those with clearly exposed movements will be at risk.

Options when running originals

In these circumstances, more research is required into identifying causes of wear, effects of lubrication, etc.; both horological and conservation texts on this subject are notable by their absence (Good 1978; Bateman 1993). More research is required into whether pivot polishing really does reduce friction at the bearings. Alternatives to conventional methods of plugging pivot holes ought to be sought, perhaps using adhesives in the building up of worn areas rather than cutting out worn components and starting afresh. The use of sacrificial wear surfaces might be a possibility, especially at the interactive surfaces of levers and the escapement. For example, at the Museum of London, one clock is working with thin shoes adhered on to the pallet faces of the escapement, with no apparent problems. Record keeping in such circumstances is vital, since some adhesives would be at risk from certain standard cleaning methods if overhauled by a conventionally-trained restorer. However, allowance has to be made for the possible, unexpected failure of adhesives sometime in the future. Some alternative techniques for modifying bearing surfaces may appear attractive, but may be irreversible, e.g. plasma coating. Other alternative approaches, such as reducing the driving force of the clockwork mechanism by, for example, running with lighter weights to lessen the overall loading on components, can be attempted with success. However, such techniques can be time consuming and require some effort. The danger of component failure always exists when running the original, sometimes with devastating results. The application of X-rays or ultrasonic investigation might be an aid to identifying weaknesses, possibly even before dismantling.

CLEANING

Ammoniacal cleaning solutions still remain popular on account of their ease of use. The question should be asked whether clock and watch movements really need to undergo extensive tarnish removal at overhaul, particularly in those cases when the mechanism is hidden from view, or whether corrosion stabilising followed by rinsing in an organic solvent will suffice. In those cases where tarnish removal might be desired, complexing agents have been developed which might be suitable (Keenan 1984).

Greater care ought to be exercised in the mechanical cleaning of horological components. Many horological pieces have fine surface finishes, notably the brass components of marine chronometers which are at risk from vigourous mechanical cleaning. Other surfaces at risk may be less obvious but play an important role in reducing frictional wear (Roberts 1988).

Rusted blued-steel components can be conserved by careful localised mechanical cleaning; armour thus treated does remain stable, provided environmental conditions are favourable (Smith 1993).

Conservators should be considering stabler and reversible alternatives to, for example, resins in the treatment of enamel dials. Effective use has been made in the cleaning of stained cracks by applying ceramic conservation methods. Poultices of sepiolite (magnesium silicate) and laponite (a synthetic, microporous clay) containing mixed additives, including biological washing powders or complexing agents, have been successfully employed, whilst tests are to be carried out using enzymes. Such methods can, however, be repetitive and time consuming. In the case of painted dial conservation, enzymatic cleaning reagents have been successfully used to remove dirt, whilst consolidation of damaged areas has been carried out on areas of flaking paint. The result is not as restored in appearance as is customary, but this is felt to be of importance in preserving originality.

Likewise, stabler alternatives are being sought for traditional lacquers. As acrylics, for example Paraloid B72, are very stable, it is likely that their removal should not pose too much difficulty in the future, whilst there is evidence that acrylics may offer greater protection from gases (Fox 1994). Whilst it might be argued that traditional lacquers are easier to apply, techniques are available to achieve a satisfactory appearance with acrylics.

CONCLUSION

Horological conservators need to play a fuller role in the decision making concerning care of clock and watch collections. Conservators should try to develop positive ideas that can be of use in collection display with less potential damage to the original. Whilst restoration has its place, conservation should be moving away from the captive bench-man approach, more typical of the restorer. Whilst some restorers have left excellent records, conservators must ensure that any records they produce can be coordinated, in order to prevent repeated dismantling of mechanisms for research. Training of conservators in this discipline must not occur in isolation from methods and techniques widely applied in other fields of conservation. The craft-type training - useful in developing restoration skills - can only be of limited value in conservation. Unless the emphasis of conservation training is altered, there is a real danger of producing not horological conservators, but conservative restorers.

REFERENCES

Bateman, D.A. 1993. in *The Science of Clocks and Watches*, (A.L. Rawlings), (3rd ed.) 309-10. British Horological Institute, Upton

Fox, B. 1994. No Silver Lining of CD's. *New Scientist* **141** (1909), 19

Good, R. 1978. in *Brittens Watch and Clockmakers Handbook, Dictionary and Guide,* (16th ed.) 201-4. London

Gould, R.T. 1931. *Notes made during re assembly of H1*, presented to the Royal Observatory, Greenwich, 24 August 1946. The entry, 15 January 1931, states: 'Unfortunately in investigating matters, I broke one of the two screws securing B S to its collet.'

Griffiths, R.J. 1992. Methods of Wheel Cutting in Horology 2. *Horological Journal* **134** (10) (April 1992), 344-9

Keenan, J. 1984. *An investigation to Find Improved Cleaning Agents for Antique Brass.* unpublished BSc Dissertation, Thames Polytechnic

Roberts, K. 1988. *Joseph Ives, Connecticut Clockmaker.* Lecture given to Antiquarian Horological Society, 24 March 1988

Smith, R.D. 1993. The Blueing and Browning of Coloured Iron and Steel. Paper given at the conference *The Conservation of Coloured Surface Treatments on Metals.* UKIC, 4 October 1993

White, G. 1989. *English Lantern Clocks.* Antique Collectors Club, Woodbridge, Suffolk

CHANGING TASTE IN THE RESTORATION OF PAINTINGS

David Bomford
National Gallery, Trafalgar Square, London WC2N 5DN

CLEANING AND RETOUCHING

In the recurring debate about the cleaning of paintings, it is not generally acknowledged that the retouching of a damaged painting has as profound an effect on its appearance as the initial cleaning. It is this narrow, specific interpretation of restoration - in the sense of retouching or inpainting - that is to be considered here, with the hope of demonstrating that critical responses to pictures are conditioned as much by what restorers have added as by what they have taken away. For while it is true that the cleaning stage is inherent with the greater possibility of irreversible change, it is also true that many complaints of unsympathetic cleaning have arisen from the way in which a painting has been retouched or not retouched. This was succinctly pointed out by Sheldon Keck over thirty years ago:

> The conservator who treats a painting often finds himself publicly criticized for overcleaning by influential people blindly ignorant of the 'actual' state of the painting. If they see it in the actual state with overpaint and varnish removed, abrasions, scars and losses visible they refuse to believe that the painting, as they previously knew it, was not in a perfect and original condition. The conservator together with his institution bears the serious blame for what is alleged to be incompetent and ruinous cleaning. If, however, he completely compensates for losses and abrasions, his critics are much more likely to remain silent even though they still prefer the former repainted and discoloured state (Keck 1963).

In fact, the two processes are inextricably linked. Except for rare examples in a perfect state, all paintings of previous centuries have sustained some loss or damage from normal ageing, accident or mistreatment. Generally, such losses will have been disguised by retouching or repainting and the picture revarnished, perhaps several times. Therefore, a restorer who is required to clean a 'typical' Old Master painting is confronted with a multi-layered structure of dirt and discoloured varnish superimposed on a retouched or repainted, damaged original. Moreover, repaint often covers large amounts of original paint around the damage it was put on to conceal and invariably discolours with time, causing unsightly dark patches below the yellowed varnish and grey dirt.

A restorer faced with such a painting has a number of options. Firstly: do nothing. Provided the picture is structurally sound it can be left alone; this option leaves the paint surface obscured by discoloured varnish and retouchings. Secondly: clean partially or selectively. The varnish can be thinned and lightened, but this might still leave darkened retouchings in place; alternatively varnish and/or retouchings can be removed in some areas but not others. Thirdly: remove all discoloured varnish and retouchings. This will reveal the paint surface and expose hitherto concealed damages.

It has to be stressed that, providing the cleaning process does not itself cause damage, all these options are valid, depending on the aesthetic objectives of the restorer, curator, or owner. However, the end results will look very different; as Cesare Brandi said, every cleaning is an act of critical interpretation (Brandi 1963).

How a painting is cleaned determines whether or how it will then be retouched. Generally speaking, the more complete the cleaning, the more old damage is revealed and the more retouching is done. No approach to cleaning eliminates the need for retouching a damaged painting altogether. Even the no-cleaning option may leave disturbing old retouchings under the varnish that have to be lightened by scumbling new paint on top of the varnish to restore some semblance of pictorial unity. This is also the case for partially or selectively cleaned paintings.

More often than not, when old paintings are cleaned, discoloured varnishes and dirt are removed entirely, together with old retouchings. Retouchings are generally retained only when they cannot be removed safely, cannot be improved upon, or can form a satisfactory basis for new retouching.

To confront a cleaned but unrestored painting is to confront one of the standard dilemmas of paintings conservation. On the one hand, the art historian needs to know how much of a painting is original and, on the other hand, the viewer of a work of art wishes to see an image uninterrupted by loss and damage. The first might be termed the historical or academic requirement, the second, the aesthetic requirement. The restoration of paintings - in the sense of retouching - is nowadays concerned with finding some compromise between these two requirements.

PRE TWENTIETH-CENTURY ATTITUDES

Analysing approaches to retouching in terms of two such conflicting requirements is a relatively modern rationale, dating only from the mid-twentieth century. Before the twentieth century, retouching had a single, simple objective: to make a painting look as good as possible in accordance with the wishes of the owner and restorer. The primary function of retouching might have been to conceal damages, but it was also used inventively to change whole passages of painting to conform to notions of contemporary taste. It is well known that the painter-restorers of past centuries considered it quite normal and unremarkable not only to repaint damages much more extensively than necessary, but also to paint over entire images that were not damaged at all, for no other reason than to impose their own taste upon the work of an earlier master.

It would be a mistake, however, to assume that, widespread though they were, such activities were ever accepted entirely uncritically. Vasari, for example, tells us in his life of Signorelli that the *Circumcision* of 1491 became damaged by damp and that the Child was repainted by the painter Sodoma. Signorelli's painting, we are told, had been of great beauty, but the Child now was 'much less beautiful than before'. Then, in a sentence that could serve as a text for a number of later writers on the subject, Vasari says, 'in truth it would sometimes be better to leave works half spoiled when they have been made by men of excellence, rather than to have them retouched by inferior masters' (Vasari 1568). It is interesting to examine modern reactions to this story. His contemporaries may well have shared Vasari's disquiet; but now, a detached historical perspective allows a less critical view and the *Circumcision* is simply regarded as a unique work by two hands.

Vasari's criticism probably represents a wider unease with restoration practices that were already prevalent in the sixteenth century. Writing in 1557, Lodovico Dolce describes the restoration of some Raphael frescoes in the Pope's palace that had been damaged by fire during the sack of Rome in 1527. Clement VII asked Sebastiano del Piombo to restore some of the Raphael heads. Later, Titian, on a visit to Rome, was shown the restorations by Sebastiano himself but, unaware of the restorer's identity, questioned angrily who had had the presumption to defile the work of so great a master (Dolce 1557).

There is a great deal of documentary evidence detailing the restoration of paintings by later painters. It is tempting to assume, as Vasari did, that it was always the fate of great paintings to be restored by lesser painters, but in the seventeenth and eighteenth centuries it was increasingly one of the functions of the great court painters to direct, and often to carry out, restorations on their masters' collections. We know, for example, that Rubens, on his first diplomatic mission to the court of Philip III of Spain in 1603, took with him as gifts sixteen copies by Pietro Facchetti after Raphael masterpieces in Rome. During the road journey from Alicante to Valladolid, they were damaged by torrential rain and Rubens, brushing aside all offers of help from local painters to assist with restoration or provide new pictures, undertook all the retouching himself. He restored all but the two most badly damaged, for which he himself painted replacements (Jaffé 1977).

Also at the Spanish court, Velazquez and Alonso Cano had responsibility for the collections of Philip IV - and Cano, at least, restored many Venetian canvases after a fire at the Buen Retiro palace in 1640 (Wethey 1955). In the eighteenth century, Mengs restored a large number of paintings in Madrid for Charles III, whose court painter he was.

Methods of restoring paintings are described in many painting treatises from medieval times onwards and, from the eighteenth century, also in handbooks on restoration. Earlier treatises usually focus on washing or cleaning pictures with a variety of potentially disastrous techniques. Increasingly, though, the question of retouching arises and, with it, the sort of reservations that Vasari had voiced over the Signorelli. Writing in 1681, Filippo Baldinucci doubts whether, for great paintings, retouching should be done at all: 'There have been many who were by no means inexperienced in matters of art and who held that the best paintings should never be retouched either much or little, by whoever it may be. For it was difficult for the restoration, be it small or large, not to show up sooner or later, however small it may have been, and it is also true that a painting that is not untouched is also very much discredited.' (Gombrich 1962)

By the late-eighteenth century, discussions about the problems of retouching were commonplace. For example, in the *Encyclopédie Méthodique: Beaux-arts* (1791) the difficulty of well-matched retouchings subsequently altering is examined, together with the desirability of confining retouching to the losses only. In the *Manuel du Peintre et du Sculpteur* by L.C. Arsenne (1833) the texturing of fillings is suggested by pressing canvas of similar weave into the still soft putty. On a less ethical note, *De la Restauration des Tableaux* by Jean Bedotti (1837) gives alarming instructions for the repainting of worn areas followed by patination of the entire area with soot.

One of the key nineteenth-century handbooks dealing with the restoration of paintings was *Il Restauratore dei Dipinti* by G. Secco-Suardo. Critical of most previous authors on the subject, he nevertheless says much that is pertinent. He reserves the terms 'restauro' and 'restauro pittorico' specifically for retouching and affirms that, whatever restorers may claim, neither exact imitation nor permanence is possible. He too, warns against excessive retouching which 'covers the very parts which should serve as a model' and of retouching in oil, since it will continue to darken: instead, he recommends water-colour or tempera (Secco-Suardo 1866, 1873).

At the same time as writers were rationalising their ideals of restoration practice in print, real restorations were proceeding apace in painters' and restorers' studios. If one era were to be identified in which restoration, in the full pejorative sense of the word, was at its height, the mid-nineteenth century would be chosen - that age of obfuscation when even the legs of furniture were hidden for fear of indecency.

It was an age in which prevailing ideas of taste toned down, covered up, disguised and altered paintings in ways that could be trivial or fantastic. The famous golden glow of toned 'gallery varnish' went hand-in-hand with over-restoration and outrageous invention. The one sustained campaign of 'modern' picture-cleaning - by Eastlake at the National Gallery - met with fierce criticism and vituperation and led to the Parliamentary Select Committee of 1853.

It has become apparent that even Eastlake's apparent commitment to unobscured pictures was deeply ambivalent. In front of the 1853 committee, the amount of cleaning and restoration was carefully played down - even to the extent of claiming that no retouching was necessary since the cleaning never reached the surface of the pictures. Speaking of one painting, the restorer John Seguier said: 'If that picture was stripped of its varnish I do not know what would be the consequence; I imagine that a vast number of repairs would come out and dreadfully disfigure it and it would be necessary to have an artist restore it.' (Brommelle 1956)

Eastlake, wary of controversy at home, increasingly had newly acquired paintings restored in Italy before adding them to the National Gallery collection. In Italy, as Alfred Stevens the painter observed, restoration could be carried out on a lavish scale, 'generally extending the colours over the sound portions of a picture in order to make the repairs less visible' (Brommelle 1956). Radical cleaning led to maximum exposure of old damages and hence to radical retouching, and Eastlake thus became involved with the most radical retoucher of all, his preferred restorer abroad, Giuseppe Molteni, *Conservatore* at the Brera, Milan.

A great deal is known about the activities of Molteni from the researches of Jaynie Anderson in recent years (Anderson 1987, 1990). Giovanni Morelli said of him: '... he is a truly outstanding restorer ... but he occasionally takes part, just as the excellent Director of the National Gallery [Eastlake] often does, in the battle ... to correct the naive inaccuracies of the Old Masters.' Molteni certainly corrected extensive naivetes in a number of National Gallery paintings, but, to his credit, he was generally honest about it, describing the alterations quite openly in letters and documents. In recent years, cleaning some of these paintings has confirmed the accuracy of his descriptions (Anderson 1987).

Some of his most inventive restorations were on admittedly ruined paintings. The famous image of *Sultan Mehmet II* by Gentile Bellini, bought by Layard 'of Nineveh' in 1865 for just £5, is revealed by x-rays to be massively damaged and its present appearance is almost wholly Molteni's work. Pisanello's *Virgin and Child with SS George and Anthony Abbot* was also restored by Molteni, who was so pleased with his own work that he considered changing his name from Giuseppe to Vittore (then thought to be Pisanello's). Its apparently perfect state is contradicted by entries in the notebook of Eastlake who bought it for his own collection: 'the blue sky is almost rubbed to the ground ... the armour and dress of St George, once beautifully finished but now almost totally obliterated' (Eastlake 1858). It stayed with Molteni for four years, so we can assume that he reworked it substantially and that much of its present appearance is due to him.

In other cases, he simply 'improved' well-preserved paintings, correcting the sitter's shoulders in Moroni's portrait of *Count Lupi*, transforming an obtrusive cow's head into white drapery in Romanino's *S. Alessandro Altarpiece*, shifting legs and feet around in Melone's *Walk to Emmaus*, and many more.

The late twentieth-century view of these restorations is pretty benign. Molteni did no harm to paintings. In his own odd way, he was reasonably ethical - documenting his work and using reversible retouching materials; and he has provoked amusement at his conceits and admiration at his skill in those who have discovered the extent of his improvisations.

TWENTIETH-CENTURY PURITANISM AND COMPROMISE

The excesses of nineteenth-century restoration caused a severe reaction in the first part of the twentieth century. By the 1920s, both art historians and restorers were claiming that retouching of any kind was an unacceptable intrusion into a painter's work, however damaged it was (Bauer-Bolton 1914). At the 1930 International Conference of Restorers in Rome, proposals were put forward that art curators should educate the public by exhibiting paintings in a damaged state. Highly impractical suggestions were also made, such as dividing collections into two - one part with damages showing for the art historian, and the rest fully restored for the public: how it was to be decided which paintings went into which half was never made clear.

The most puritanical views of all were expressed at the 20th International Congress of the History of Art in New York in 1961. In a session devoted to the aesthetic and historical aspects of the presentation of damaged pictures, the art historian Richard Offner stated the purist case:

> a work of art can be organic only so long as it is the product of a single personality. Any restoration that introduces paint or shape within its boundaries - even if the restoration be limited to the missing portions alone - must prove intolerable. ... The rejection of all but its original

elements is the first and final condition of an adequate restoration of a painting. Fragmentary as the result would be, it would nevertheless give as the maximum that the damage in the original work would admit. It would, moreover, draw the faculties of the spectator explicitly and exclusively to an unadulterated object and its own artistic qualities. (Offner 1963)

Speaking later, the art historian Millard Meiss said, rather loftily:

> blank areas of uniform colour produce a critical shock ... uncultivated beholders, or those who look on the run do not survive the first shock. For those who do, the original shines far more brightly. The unreconstructed lacunae remain, of course, obtrusive, ugly shapes. Indeed they must retain a considerable degree of discreteness; otherwise, in the process of perception they will merge with the surviving areas and contaminate our response. (Meiss 1963).

'The chief reason for the problem', said Offner in his paper, presumably without the faintest trace of irony, 'is to be sought in the universal greed for completeness ... people find it hard to tolerate the absence of legs, arms and heads or other disruptions in the continuity of a composition.' Offner had clearly been enraged at a previous paper by Philip Hendy, then Director of the London National Gallery, who had given a slick, sophisticated and, perhaps, cynical defence of his decision to buy Giorgione's *Il Tramonto* (which had several large holes, invisibly mended) and to exhibit it alongside technical photographs showing its true but now hidden condition:

> there is an immense difference in effect upon morale [said Hendy] between the sight of a picture stripped, and that of photographs showing it in that condition exhibited alongside a picture which looks as good as the restorer can make it. In the first case, the reaction would be a high percentage of bewilderment and disgust and no percentage whatever of enjoyment. In the second case, as much enjoyment as can now be got from the picture plus a surprising amount of appreciation of the restorer's art. With the second procedure, we may be said to have given all the facts but not the whole truth. Or did we show more of the truth by demonstrating not only the extent of the damage, but also the extent to which it could be made good?

Hendy's main conclusion is that the unity of every picture must be preserved: 'We must not forget that a very little damage can make a very great wreck.' (Hendy 1963)

By the 1960s, compromise retouching solutions were in vogue - up to a point: everybody talked about them, many attempted them, but very few did them well. Helmut Ruhemann was later to say: 'In the various galleries which have adopted the policy of visible retouching I have seen very few satisfactory examples of it, but innumerable offensive ones. It needs more talent, skill and taste to produce a good compromise than a good matching reconstruction.' (Ruhemann 1968)

Ruhemann had been one of the first restorers to propose various forms of visible retouching (Ruhemann 1931). At one extreme, satisfying the needs of historical integrity, would be actual holes in the fabric of the painting. At the other would be perfectly matched retouching. In between would be a range of compromise solutions - and Ruhemann listed as many as sixteen ways of rendering inpainting discreet yet discrete. These involved use of so-called 'neutral' tones (although in reality no single colour can appear neutral and unaffected by the different colours that surround it), stippled colours, outlining of missing forms, omission of craquelure, manipulation of fillings, texturing of paint, and so on. Few of these ideas were pursued, but a particular genre of visible retouching did become widely practised in Italy and is still commonly used there. Pioneered by Cesare Brandi (Brandi 1953) and perfected by Paolo and Laura Mora at the Istituto Centrale del Restauro, Rome, its first manifestation - known as *tratteggio* or *rigatini* - was the system of reconstructing missing parts using regular vertical brush strokes: colours could be matched and forms reconstructed, but the vertical striping remained visible. This was a much admired technique, allowing a close approximation of pictorial unity while leaving inpaintings visible on close inspection. The problem was that it is exceedingly difficult to do well and, while it is well suited to earlier Italian paintings, it is less appropriate for other types of picture. Its effective use has, therefore, been limited to a small number of skilled practitioners and a particular school of painting.

Since the introduction of *tratteggio*, Florentine adaptations of the technique have become more widely practised. In the first, known as 'chromatic selection', brushstrokes can follow forms, and colour combinations are made by juxtaposing primary or secondary colours and allowing them to mix optically. The other variant is called 'chromatic abstraction' and is intended for areas of loss too large for forms to be satisfactorily reconstructed. Here a mesh of brushstrokes is applied across the loss, using the three primaries and black - the balance of the colours being derived from the adjacent original colours (Baldini 1978; Casazza 1981).

Brandi's original intention was to devise an all embracing theory of restoration (Brandi 1963). He divided the life of a work of art into its creation and its subsequent history. As it ages, various processes of alteration begin, and these can also be divided into those that enhance our view of the work as a precious cultural object of a venerable age and those that detract from this perception. The aim of restoration is to leave the positive, desirable changes (such as the craquelure) but to suppress the negative, undesirable ones, without actually eliminating their presence altogether. Hence the adoption of the *tratteggio* method. Brandi employed *Gestalt* theory to analyse the overall appearance of paintings as phenomena greater than the sum of their individual parts. He had hoped that restoration could also be analysed in purely theoretical terms, but soon realised that, by its very nature, it had to be empirical and dealt with case by case. This empiricism led to the dilution of the intellectual rigour of *tratteggio* into its less satisfactory variants. The very evident danger of chromatic selection and abstraction - and, indeed, of other forms of visible retouching - is that, badly done, they can become mystifying and distracting design elements in their own right, catching the eye and subverting their intended function.

IS RESTORATION ACCEPTABLE?

The problem of how and how much to restore damaged paintings will continue to be a matter of debate. Notions of taste will always play their part. There will always be those who argue for no retouching at all, or compromise retouchings, although in recent years the consensus has swung back towards more or less deceptive reconstruction. Even with fully matched retouching, it should be realised that there are widely differing expectations of how much restoration should be done - how 'finished' the painting should look, how much it has undergone what in Italian is termed *ripristino*.

Clearly, Brandi's positive, desirable aspects of ageing, such as the craquelure, should not be suppressed, but a restorer might nevertheless sometimes consider it necessary to retouch particularly disturbing cracks. Worn paint is more problematic; passages of wearing can clearly disrupt the legibility of a composition, but too diligent a restoration can give a misleading idea of a painting's condition and impart a uniformity out of sympathy with the original surface. It is often said that the most important quality in a good restorer is knowing when to stop. Even in a fully matched restoration it is unnecessary - indeed undesirable - to retouch every blemish; the aim is not pristine perfection, but a unified image that nevertheless shows its age.

Whatever the type and extent of a restoration, there are some fundamental principles which must be observed if the restoration is to be acceptable. Firstly, materials used for retouching should be reversible - that is, removable by means that do not endanger the original paint. The restorer is faced with a paradox here, because although reversibility is vital, durability and stability are also desirable; materials that are going to discolour badly or break down are clearly unacceptable. In practice, this narrows the choice of retouching media to a few synthetic resins, water colour and egg tempera, provided it is applied over an isolating varnish. Oil paint is not suitable for retouching.

Secondly, there must be some way of distinguishing original paint from retouching. This should ideally involve recording the condition of the paint before retouching by photography, together with reports describing the condition and the materials used, and also, in some cases, the use of visible or compromise retouchings. In any case, no retouching is ever so perfect that it cannot be detected under magnification.

The third principle is that retouching should be confined only to areas of damage. This requirement is the origin of the descriptive term 'inpainting', which implies painting within the boundaries of a loss. One cannot strictly enunciate this principle as 'retouching should never cover original paint', since it often does, for example, in the case of wearing, where fragmentary upper layers might be relinked over existing underpaint. It is better to say that none of the original that was intended to be seen should be concealed.

Quite how much reconstruction of missing areas in a damaged painting is possible can only be decided in individual cases, using internal evidence, copies, related paintings, prints, and so on. If a loss cannot be reconstructed without undue invention, then fully matched retouching should not be attempted.

It is difficult to match colours and retouch accurately if the surface of a painting is still obscured by old varnish and other retouchings. This observation has been used to justify a possible corollary of our third principle: since a restoration must be strictly confined to areas of damage and not conceal surrounding paint, it follows that everything else that confuses or conceals the original should be removed. 'All retouchings' said Philip Hendy 'must be done in the full knowledge of the exact local colour and original appearance, in so far as it has come down to us, of the whole picture under treatment.' (Hendy 1963)

Even this simple statement cannot be viewed unequivocally. Conservators and curators are now much more wary of declaring a belief in absolutes, especially in an area as sensitive as the cleaning of paintings. The conclusion can only be that, for damaged paintings, every cleaning determines how a painting is restored, and every restoration informs a view of the initial cleaning. At both stages the restorer acts as an intermediary between the painting with all its physical changes and the observer. Both cleaning and restoration are acts of critical interpretation and, as has been seen, both can involve widely different philosophies. There are no absolutes any more in the aesthetics of restoring paintings, only relativities - no objective truths, only subjective ones. Provided ethical principles have been observed, whether or not a particular restoration is acceptable is a matter for individual taste and judgement.

ACKNOWLEDGEMENTS

I would like to thank Jill Dunkerton for help with Italian sources and Zahira Véliz for tactful criticism.

REFERENCES

Anderson, J. 1987. Layard and Morelli. in Acts of Symposium *Austen Henry Layard tra l'Oriente e Venezia* (held at Venice 1983) (ed. Fales and Hickey), 109-37. Rome

Anderson, J. 1990. The First Cleaning Controversy at the National Gallery 1846-1853. in *Appearance, Opinion, Change*, 3-7. UKIC, London

Arsenne, L.C. 1833. *Manuel du Peinture et du Sculpteur*. (2 vols.) Paris

Baldini, U. 1978. *Teoria del Restauro e unita di Metodologia*. Florence

Bauer-Bolton, V. 1914. *Sollen fehlende Stellen bei Gemälden ergänzt werden?* Munich

Bedotti, J. 1837. *De la restauration des tableaux*. Paris

Brandi, C. 1953. Il restauro e l'interpretazione dell'opera d'Arte. in *Atti del Seminario di Storia dell' Arte*, I-XVI

Brandi, C. 1963. *Teoria del Restauro*. Rome

Brommelle, N. 1956. Materials for a History of Conservation. *Studies in Conservation*, **2**, 175-88

Casazza, O. 1981. *Il Restauro Pittorico nell'unita di Metodologia*. Florence

Dolce, L. 1557. *Dialogo della Pittura intitolato l'Aretino*. Vinegia

Eastlake, 1858. Notebook in National Gallery, London, archives

Gombrich, E. 1962. Dark Varnishes: Variations on a Theme of Pliny. *The Burlington Magazine*, **CIV**, 51-5

Hendy, P. 1963. Taste and Science in the Presentation of Damaged Pictures. in *Studies in Western Art: Problems of the 19th and 20th Centuries*, 139-45. Princeton

Jaffé, M. 1977. *Rubens and Italy*, 67-8. Oxford

Keck, S. 1963. Discussion session in *Studies in Western Art: Problems of the 19th and 20th centuries*, 170-5. Princeton

Meiss, M. 1963. Discussion session in *Studies in Western Art: Problems of the 19th and 20th centuries*, 163-6. Princeton

Offner, R. 1963. Restoration and Conservation. in *Studies in Western Art: Problems of the 19th and 20th Centuries*, 152-62. Princeton

Parliamentary Select Committee, 1853. *The Report from the Select Committee on the National Gallery together with the 'Minutes' of Evidence*. The House of Commons, 4 August 1853

Ruhemann, H. 1931. La technique de la conservation des tableaux. *Mouseion*, **XV** (3), 14-23

Ruhemann, H. 1968. *The Cleaning of Paintings*. London

Secco-Suardo, G. 1866, 1873. *Il Restauratore dei Dipinti*. (2 vols.) Milan, (combined ed. Milan 1918)

Vasari, G. 1568. *Vita di Luca Signorelli*. 1913 ed. and trans. G. de Vere, vol.iv, 72. London

Wethey, H. 1955. *Alonso Cano*, 47. Princeton

RESTORATION OF ART ON PAPER IN THE WEST: A CONSIDERATION OF CHANGING ATTITUDES AND VALUES

Joanna M. Kosek

Department of Conservation, The British Museum, London WC1B 3DG

INTRODUCTION

The word 'restoration' can be defined as the process of bringing an object back to a former or original state. In the conservation of Western works of art on paper, the term tends to be used within the profession with some inaccuracy to denote a range of activities which have the general aim of 'improving' the appearance of a damaged print or drawing. Rather than returning a work to its original or former state, restoring means in this instance imposing on the damaged print or drawing some aesthetic cohesion such as has been subjectively decided by the owner, trustee and/or restorer.

In practice, restoration of prints and drawings includes such activities as flattening, removal of previous repairs and reconstructions, removal of stains, bleaching, repairing and reconstructing missing areas, retouching and overdrawing or overpainting.

The physical aspect of restoration work is usually straightforward, although the degree, skill and precision with which individual measures have been carried out over the centuries have varied greatly. Far less obvious are the motives for undertaking restoration and attitudes towards the objects themselves.

This paper attempts to look at the restoration of prints and drawings in the West from an historical perspective, but, of course, has no claim to being all-encompassing. It focuses on attitudes to prints and drawings, gives examples of early and more recent restorations, refers to published statements, and points to possible reasons behind approaches to restoration within a broader cultural context.

A restricting factor in this investigation is the problem of attributing a date to early restorations, as well as the difficulty of being able to examine a sufficient number of artefacts to allow for generalisations, especially since the survival of a given restoration down to our times is often a matter of accident, while an example of restoration might simply escape detection.

THE BEGINNINGS

Restoration of works of art on paper in the West would properly have started at the time of the first manufacture of paper in Europe in the twelfth century, assuming that a desire to repair and make things look their best is natural, and that people will always have carried out such work on their objects. However, apart from some 'housekeeping' measures, little evidence is available to show what, if any, restoration was carried out on the earliest drawings and prints on paper.

The first drawings on paper which were not dependant on an accompanying text followed a long tradition of medieval codices and model books on parchment. Such books consisted of motifs noted down as reference material and as an aid in future compositions. Drawings were protected by bindings, and fulfilled a utilitarian function, unlike the illustrations in illuminated manuscripts. Successive artists would not have hesitated to make alterations or additions, treating codices as their own material. Needless to say this would not have been done with expensively-produced illuminations in manuscripts.

Printmaking starts in Europe towards the end of the fourteenth century with woodcuts produced as cheap devotional objects, the majority of which perished through daily use (Mayor 1980, 5-13).

THE RENAISSANCE PERIOD

The didactic function of drawing persisted and prevailed during the Renaissance. Drawing was primarily a means of training, and studying from a model and copying occupied most of an artist's apprenticeship.

Beginning perhaps with the fifteenth century, however, drawing became more than a simple manifestation of craftsmanship, but rather began to emerge as a form of artistic expression (Sciola 1992, 1-14). Drawings became more experimental and individualistic and sometimes highly elaborate and finished. Whether appreciated as sources for ideas and images or admired on a more intellectual level, drawings were kept almost exclusively by artists and patrons (e.g. presentation drawings) and with few exceptions (Ames-Lewis 1982, 3) received no broader public attention.

Loose prints and drawings must have always been very vulnerable. Those protected by bindings stood more of a chance of surviving. An example here might be the sketchbook of Jacopo Bellini (c.1400-c.1470) (BM P&D 1855-8-11-(1...98)) consisting of 98 paper leaves. This bears no signs of restoration, and has survived in remarkably good condition.

At the same time painting and sculpture enjoyed quite a different status. Generous commissions resulted in the production of a wealth of major works. As with medieval manuscripts, costly objects were well protected and well looked-after.

In an unprecedented way the Renaissance also lavished its protection on objects surviving from the Antique. These were sought out, excavated, collected with great enthusiasm, and inevitably restored.

Popes and princes competed in exhibiting their collections, as these would lend publicity to their wealth and power, and to the objects themselves. Damaged sculptures that had been excavated were subjected to some restoration. It is noteworthy that even then with important objects or collections this restoration work was discussed and disputed. In one such dispute, Michelangelo himself argued for the 'untouchability' of his own and antique works of art (Taschini 1943, 18 quoted after Rymaszewski 1992, 16).

Prints and drawings, in contrast, were not the subject of such concern. On the whole, their status did not equal that of highly finished and expensive productions. Many drawings in particular must have been disposed of or destroyed by the artist himself in order not to disclose his working methods. This was the case, for example, with many sketches by Michelangelo (Ames-Lewis 1982, 11-12).

Prints and drawings also served as a record of imaginary restorations or reconstructions of antique sculptures (Haskell and Penny 1981, 21). Although they were used as tools in this intellectual game of 'restoration' there is little evidence that restoration was applied to prints or drawings themselves.

FIRST COLLECTIONS

During the Renaissance and the Baroque, the fashion for collecting and the progress of Antiquarianism led to the first assemblages of prints and drawings. The bulk of graphic art was kept primarily as rarities or as encyclopaedic, and later art-historical reference material. It was stored in bound volumes, in cabinet drawers and portfolios, in bundles or even in frames in '*il camerino*', '*das*

Wunderkammer', '*das Kunstkammer*', or as part of a library. Since graphic art was collected primarily for reference and not intended for display, damaged prints and drawings probably escaped attempts at 'improving' their appearance.

Lack of particular interest in condition can be observed in the first collections of prints. In the late sixteenth-century collection of Ferdinand Archduke of Tyrol, for example, there is no real concern for the quality of printed impressions or uniqueness (Parshall 1982, 178). His album of Dürer prints and drawings constitutes an exception. It demonstrates the exclusive position of some individual works, i.e. drawings by renowned artists and prints by *peintre-graveurs* such as Dürer, Mantegna or Marcantonio Raimondi which had always been highly esteemed and valued by connoisseurs. On the whole, however, in late Renaissance collections, demand for quantity in visual information seems to overshadow the issue of quality. This tendency was encouraged and exploited by publishing firms, especially in Rome and Antwerp (Parshall 1982, 178).

Some of the first known examples of restoration of drawings can be found in Giorgio Vasari's (1511-1574) *Libro de'Disegni*. Vasari built up a collection of drawings consisting of five volumes representing contemporary and earlier artists. In assembling and mounting this collection, drawings were frequently trimmed to fit elaborate architectural mounts and pasted down on album sheets. Worn-out drawings were sometimes retouched or overdrawn. In other cases the size of the drawings was increased and missing areas were restored to fit the format by matching the colour of the background of the drawing directly on the album sheet. Borderlines were then drawn along the edge of the original and the repair. More interesting here are instances where Vasari cut out an original sheet outside the outlines of the drawing and incorporated it within the design of his mount, as if he cared only for the drawn lines as representing the artist's idea, disregarding the value of the support. In a page of drawings from the Florentine School now in the Chatsworth Collection, drawings cut out in such a manner were adhered to the album page and embedded in clouds drawn by Vasari. These additions are perhaps more likely to be imaginary than reconstructive restoration.

This process of subordinating drawings to the dictates of an album is not dissimilar to arranging and altering antique sculptures to fit the interior of papal and princely gardens and palaces (Haskell and Penny 1981, 7-15).

Such restoration, which aimed at blending a drawing within an album page or mount involving simple reconstruction or enhancement of the image by overdrawing, has been very common and can be found also today. The operation might have been executed with greater or lesser precision and sensitivity, and often involved trimming the original, but it was not meant to be 'invisible', or to conceal a damaged area.

Interest in the condition of prints becomes popular amongst the seventeenth-century collectors (Parshall 1982, 143) and is to be observed already in such early collections as the Mannerist collection of Cassiano dal Pozzo (1588-1657). It is further confirmed by Abraham Bosse (1602-76) in his *Sentiments sur la Distinction des diverses Manières de Peinture, Dessein & Graveure ...* of 1649, where the author instructs print connoisseurs on the choice of rare and early impressions. (The latter in particular had been generally less valued previously.) Bosse emphasises the value of good condition and specifically advocates choosing prints on 'very white' paper (Stevenson 1990, 422).

Not surprisingly, one of the first written instructions concerning the restoration of prints and drawings, which is found in *Pictoria sculptoria et quae subalternarum artium spectantia*, an art manual by Théodore De Mayerne (1573-1655), mentions methods for restoring 'lustre' and the colour of discoloured or stained prints. These methods, such as sun-bleaching or sizing in animal glue, derive from papermaking (Stevenson 1990, 422).

Although successful chemical treatments remain difficult to detect, mechanical intervention such as repairs or overpainting will be much less so. A fascinating account of the seventeenth-century practice of retouching drawings was discovered by Catherine Monbeig Goguel in her investigation of the collection of the German financier Everard Jabach (1618-1695) (Goguel 1989).

RETOUCHING BY ARTISTS

Beginning with the seventeenth century there survive numerous examples where an individual artist may be seen retouching other artists' work. Well-known cases are the drawings overdrawn by Rubens, or at a later date, by Boucher and Natoire.

Rubens is known to have retouched drawings by Dürer, Giovanni da Udine, Giulio Romano, Francesco Salviati and Caravaggio. It appears from the records of the sale of the drawings that Rubens' intervention increased the contemporary commercial value of the drawings.

In the seventeenth and eighteenth centuries, artists were trained in copying and imitating well-known Masters, and these skills (which included retouching) were highly appreciated (Goguel 1989). Retouching original drawings was not only a means of restoring or enhancing their appeal, but also a way of studying an artist's hand. Both Rubens and Rembrandt are known to have used such methods (Sciola 1992, 96-7).

Today an extensive group of retouched drawings can be found within the original collection of Louis XIV housed in the Louvre, which itself came from that gathered by Jabach. It appears that the latter employed artists to copy drawings in his collections and to retouch damaged or faded ones.

Drawings were appreciated and valued according to how highly finished they were. This is apparent from the way in which they were priced for the royal purchaser. The highly finished drawings from Jabach's collection were priced at 157,000 livres for 2621, while small items with 'little enough work and less finish' were sold at the contrasting price of 19,345 livres for 2911 (Goguel 1989, 828). As expected the drawings which had been retouched for Jabach belonged to the former group. Restoration was performed here to deceive, but despite this it was not regarded as outright forgery.

THE EIGHTEENTH CENTURY

A major development in the appreciation of prints and drawings makes itself felt at the end of the seventeenth century and the beginning of the eighteenth, and is the immediate result of the growing attitude that prints and drawings could be finished art objects in their own right and could be displayed as works of art and as decorative objects.

As an illustration of this shift in attitude, one thinks of the artist Giovanni Battista Piazzetta (1683-1754) or the pastellist Rosalba Carriera (1675-1757), who earned more through drawings tailored to the market than did many contemporary painters with their oils.

It became popular to mount, glaze and frame graphic art, which was facilitated by developments in the production of glass where the casting of sheet glass was perfected by 1700 (Logan 1951, 21). Framed prints and drawings were an essential feature of the intimate apartments of the nobility and *nouveau riche*. The fashion might have been set by the great collectors and dealers in prints and drawings themselves. The Parisian house of Pierre-Jean Mariette (1694-1774) in rue St-Jacques, for example, was decorated with framed drawings in characteristic blue mounts (Scott 1973, 58).

Mariette is renowned for the quality of his collected drawings, his scholarly approach to artistic contributions and also the pedantry of his presentation of the collection. Prior to his mounting (which involved adhering the drawing to a card mount), Mariette carefully restored drawings (Sciola 1992, 139). An example of such work might be Raphael's *Study for a Soldier in a Resurrection* (BM P&D 1854-5-13-11). The restoration involved making up the torn-off area by adhering a piece of similar paper and partly reconstructing the missing portion. The reconstruction was carried out here with accuracy and in a style and drawing medium similar to that of the original. The reconstructed line of the arm is lighter than the original, which makes the restoration obvious, yet the finished result is subtle and sympathetic.

In the eighteenth century, growing interest in displaying prints and drawings resulted in a demand for restoration work, evidenced by the increasing number of publications recommending restorative methods for paper (Donnithorne 1988). These include such techniques as removal of oil stains (Chomel 1725), sun bleaching (Hecquet 1751), mechanical cleaning with the use of rubber (Priestly 1770), or bleaching by exposure to dew (Buc'Hoz 1783).

In these writings a sort of kitchen-table advice prevails, sometimes copied from earlier recipes, and often disclosed to the reader as 'secrets'. However, the developments in science that took place in the eighteenth century are reflected in the appearance of new vocabulary, such as 'experiments', 'methods', or 'manière', and by taking advantage of new discoveries in chemistry, such as the discovery of chlorine in 1774 (Chaptal 1787).

The culmination of this change in approach to the subject, however restricted it might have been to the more informed, are reports by the chemist Jean Antoine Chaptal of 1787, which reveal restorative treatments for paper, parchment and papyri, or the experiments in unrolling papyrus from Herculaneum by Antonio Piaggio which began in the 1750s. It is a foretaste of the greater interest in a drawing or print as an object possessing not only an aesthetic and artistic significance, but also intrinsic value as a representative of its historical milieu, materials and methods of production. Such a change in appreciation might have been influenced by the serious practical problems in conservation raised by the great archaeological discoveries of the middle of the century at Pompeii and Herculaneum (Caldararo 1987, 85).

THE NINETEENTH CENTURY

The nineteenth century witnessed a major development in the concept of restoration (Frycz 1975, 7-15). It was, of course, a period of nationalist movements and intense interest in the past: 'Our age has adopted an attitude towards the past in which it stands quite alone among historical ages.' (Viollet-le-Duc 1875, 13)

The focus of this attention was historical monuments, but it involved ramifications on all levels, and had some influence on the treatment of small works of art, paintings, sculpture, prints and drawings.

A preoccupation with historicism can be observed in the Gothic revival, followed by the Neo-Renaissance and Neo-Baroque, and the Eclectic Movement. Historicism seeps into all disciplines. Restoration which related to historicism was an important element in contemporary thinking, indeed it attained major status: 'The restoration of disfigured and decayed works of art is ... next in importance to their production.' (Field 1835, 216)

Restoration of works of art develops then as a concept and discipline. It no longer refers only to purely technical solutions but embodies something of a philosophy. It results from a real care for objects as possessing intrinsic historical value.

Two early definitions of the term 'restoration' may be adduced here from *The Shorter Oxford English Dictionary*: 'The action or process of restoring something to an unimpaired or perfect condition' (1801); 'The process of carrying out alteration or repairs with the idea of restoring a building to something like its original form' (1824).

Examples of nineteenth-century restorations of prints and drawings and the evidence found in technical literature can often be related directly to the above definitions.

One observes emphasis on the 'invisible' repair and reconstruction of the image. There exist instructions for strengthening weak impressions by washes in ink (Cumberland 1827; Slater 1897), reconstructing missing areas with matching fragments of other prints (Tuer 1882; Slater 1897), or by imitating hatched lines by careful retouching in pen and ink (Bonnardot 1858). There are detailed instructions for techniques of making an invisible repair by matching paper or using paper pulp, or by splitting original sheets (Tuer 1882).

Much literature is devoted to stain removal and the bleaching of prints and drawings (Tuer 1882). Many new methods of bleaching must have been over-enthusiastically employed by restorers as they blindly followed the advice of chemists involved in the paper and textile industries.

It seems, indeed, that paper restorers aimed at restoring prints and drawings to 'unimpaired or perfect condition' and must have taken pride in results which would have been difficult to detect at the time.

Restoration served also as a means of deception, and forging seems to have been common practice in the booming nineteenth-century market for prints and drawings. This practice has been vividly described by Andrew Tuer in his book *Bartolozzi and his Works* ... (with the explicit subtitle) *concerning some observations on the Present Demand for and Value of his Prints; the way to detect Modern Impressions from Worn-out Plates and to recognise Falsely-tinted Impressions; Deceptions attempted with Prints; Print Collection, Judging, Handling, etc.* of 1885.

The aim of thorough restoration in the name of stylistic purity, as advocated and practised by its greatest exponent, the French architect Eugène Viollet-le-Duc (1814-1879), was strongly opposed by such prominent thinkers of the century as John Ruskin (1819-1900), who warned: 'Under the name of "restoration" the ruin of noblest architecture and painting is constant through Europe.' (Ruskin 1880: 67 [Letter to the Times of 1852])

It is unlikely that every paper restorer of the nineteenth century was familiar with Ruskin's writings; however the impact of such controversy on the educated must have been considerable. It can be detected in the literature on restoration of paper, and in particular in the architect and bibliophile Alfred Bonnardot's (1804-1884) *Essai sur l'Art de Restaurer* ... first published in 1846. This is full of precise instructions concerning the restoration of paper objects. It begins, however, with an unprecedented warning against the potential danger of the removal of historical evidence in the process of removing stains: 'Before discussing the means of attacking the stains which may blemish a book or a precious print, I am going to say that in certain cases it might be very desirable to allow them to remain.' (Buck 1917, 25)

Bonnardot confesses further to a switch in his own attitude towards restoration from a desire to see a damaged object in pristine condition to regretting that a restored object had been stripped of its history (Buck 1917: 27).

TWENTIETH CENTURY

By the beginning of the twentieth century there already existed the theoretical background for an increased appreciation of the integrity of an art object. This can be observed, for example, in the work of the Austrian art historian Alois Riegl (1858-1905), a vigorous advocate of non-intervention, and Max Dvořak (1874-1921) who, in his *Katechismus der Denkmalpflege* of 1916, argued for 'conservation' as opposed to 'restoration'. In the 1960s, this issue was again addressed by another Austrian historian, Walter Frodl.

Simultaneously, one can point to progress in the scientific analysis of archaeological and art objects by scientists associated with work in museums, such as Friedrich Rathgen (1862-1942), Alexander Scott (1853-1947), Alfred Lucas (1867-1945) or Harold Plenderleith, to mention but a few. Their view of the treatment of an artefact saw a merely empirical approach replaced by one based on scientific reasons in which the treatment has to be preceded by an understanding of the chemical and physical composition of an object and of its deterioration mechanisms.

Already at the end of the nineteenth century one encounters in-depth investigation into the fading of watercolours (Russell and Abney 1888), and this approach to the analysis of deterioration phenomena has persisted to the present day.

Some of the first recorded scientific restorations of drawings are to be found in Alexander Scott's British Museum report of 1921, which concerned the removal of oil stains from a drawing by Jean Antoine Watteau (BM P&D 1846-11-14-25). The involvement of scientists in examination of objects and evaluation of treatment has also become the rule in contemporary treatments of works of art on paper. Art history, too, progressively relies on technical examination of paper and drawing media to establish provenance and authenticity of prints and drawings (e.g. Ehrlich and Neff 1973).

Additionally, emphasis is now put by art historians on the aesthetic qualities of paper (Robison 1977), as well as painting and drawing media.

The development of conservation as a discipline led to the exchange of research findings and attempts at standardisation, such as keeping records of the condition of objects and their treatment, and complying with codes of conservation ethics.

Conservation ethics has borrowed deeply from those of the medical profession resulting in the attitude that art objects, like patients, should be treated without discrimination; theoretically the same criteria apply to a cartoon by Leonardo as to an ephemeral playbill. In contrast to the medical world, however, there is no strict legislation that controls such attitudes. Restoration which is still sanctioned as treatment by codes of conservation ethics (IIC-Canadian Group 1989; IPC 1991; AIC 1993) must rely on the judgement of individuals, and is applied in each case on the basis of circumstance. Its application is governed by several principles such as reversibility and accountability. Reversibility, perhaps the most important principle, is also that which is most often questioned (Smith 1987; Appelbaum 1987).

Concern about reversibility must derive from an ever-increasing conviction that minimum intervention in the treatment of works of art is the only right approach. This can make restoration a somewhat embarrassing issue, although restoration is still a major part of a paper conservator's work.

As recently remarked by Alan Donnithorne:

> Unlike many other kinds of artefact, works of art on paper are commonly subject to forms of deterioration which cause severe disfigurement. Many of these, such as stains, discolouration and foxing, permeate the whole fabric of the object, rather than merely affecting the surface. This means that remedial treatments for paper tend to be highly interventive ... . With prints and drawings we are concerned with aesthetic values as well as historic evidence, and it is a matter for informed judgement to decide on appropriate treatment which will take account of both criteria. (Donnithorne 1994)

In the British Museum, decisions about restoration of prints and drawings are taken jointly by an art historian and a conservator who can also consult a scientist. Damaged, disfigured and abused prints and drawings are often subjected to some measure of restoration. Partial restoration is preferred, such as flattening paper without complete elimination of creases, partial removal of stains or discolourations to make them less intrusive, or toning down repairs to a colour lighter than that of the background. Retouching an original is virtually never practised. However, there are exceptional cases, such as when a stain or a recent damage greatly detracts from an image. In such a case, toning down with pastels might be considered. Old repairs, restorations or old mounts, if removed, are kept and well recorded. Many are left *in situ* as evidence, which reflects the modern tendency to preserve everything old as it is (Chamberlain 1979; Fowler 1992).

A very tidy but obvious repair is preferred, but pursuit of the 'invisible' repair (i.e. one not immediately obvious although detectable by close examination) has not been abandoned altogether.

An interesting perspective on this point is provided by the IIC-Canadian Group *Code of Ethics and Guidance for Practice of 1989* or IPC *Code of Ethics and Professional Standards* of 1991 (echoing the nineteenth-century attitude expressed by A. Tuer), which permits inconspicuous restoration provided that it is not carried out with fraudulent intent.

CONCLUSION

The twentieth century has seen 'restoration' become largely discredited and replaced by 'conservation', although the latter term is often used as a euphemism for restorative treatments.

Paper conservation literature presents technical discussion and analysis of restorative techniques, such as bleaching and stain removal, but there is far less discussion devoted to repair and reconstruction, as if the misjudgments of the nineteenth century have produced in us a sense of reticence. Instead there prevails the literature of scepticism which exposes the limitations of conservation treatments and advocates a cautious approach.

And yet paper restoration work can still capture public attention. For instance, Eric Harding's highly successful restoration of the Leonardo cartoon *The Virgin and Child with St Anne and St John the Baptist* at the National Gallery (Harding *et al* 1989; Harding and Oddy 1992) gained universal acclaim from colleagues and media alike. This involved recent damage to a prime national object, and the case confirms the approach to restoration advocated by Max Dvořak and Walter Frodl in allowing restoration which includes reconstruction, in exceptional circumstances.

Today, previous or old restorations of works of art on paper are usually considered evidence about the history of an individual object but they are, to a large extent, more of a testimony to the social phenomena related to art.

ACKNOWLEDGEMENTS

I especially wish to thank Alan Donnithorne for much information and help with the manuscript. I would also like to thank Antony Griffiths for information about early print collecting, Sandra Smith for the reference on eighteenth-century glass and my colleagues in the Museum for critical comments on the text, in particular Jenny Bescoby.

Special thanks are extended to Andrew Oddy for encouragement and for editing this paper.

REFERENCES

AIC, 1993. Code of Ethics and Guidelines for Practice. *AIC News*, September

Ames-Lewis F. 1982. *Drawing in Early Renaissance Italy*. Newhaven/London

Appelbaum, B. 1987. Criteria for Treatment: Reversibility. in *JAIC* **26**, 65-73

Bonnardot, A. 1858. *Essai sur L'Art de Restaurer les Estampes et les Livres, ou Traite sur les Meilleurs Procedes pour Blanchir, Detacher, Decolourier, Reparer, et Conserver les Estampes, Livres, et Dessins*. (2nd ed. Paris), Reprinted 1967, New York

Buc'Hoz, P.J. 1783-86. *Recueil de Secrets Surs et Experimentes a l'Usage des Artistes*. 3 vols., Paris

Buck, M.S. 1917. *Book Repair and Restoration*. Philadelphia

Caldararo, N.L. 1987. An Outline History of Conservation in Archaeology and Anthropology as presented through its Publications. *JAIC* **26,** 85-104

Chamberlain, E.R. 1979. *Preserving the Past.* London

Chaptal, J.A.C. 1787. Observations sur l'acide Muriatique Oxygenee (Chlore Liquide) applique au Blanchiment des Estampes. *Annales de Chemie,* **1,** 69

Chomel, N. 1725. *Dictionaire Oeconomique.* 2 vols., English translation by R. Bradley, London

Cumberland, G. 1827. Introductory essay (written in 1816), in *An Essay on the Utility of Collecting the Best Works of the Ancient Engravers.* London

Donnithorne, A.R. 1988. Early Approaches to the Conservation of Works of Art on Paper: Cleaning, Repair and Restoration. in *Early Advances in Conservation*, (V. Daniels ed.), 15-25. British Museum Occasional Paper No. 65

Donnithorne, A.R. 1994 forthcoming. The Conservation of Prints and Drawings at the British Museum: Policy and Practice. (Paper submitted for *S.I.M.E. Colloquium*, Paris, 1994)

Dvořak, M. 1916. *Katechismus der Denkmalpflege.* Vienna

Ehrlich, E. and Neff, J.H. 1973. *The Gott Impression of Pollaiuolo's Battle of the Nudes.* National Gallery of Art, Washington

Field, G. 1835. *Chromatography, or a Treatise on Colours and Pigments.* London

Fowler, P.J. 1992. *The Past in Contemporary Society: Then, Now.* London

Frycz, J. 1975. *Restauracje i Konserwacje Zabytków Architektury w Polsce w Latach 1795-1918.* Warsaw

Goguel, C.M. 1989. Taste and Trade: the Retouched Drawings in the Everard Jabach Collection at the Louvre. *Burlington Magazine,* **Nov** 1989, 821-35

Harding, E., Braham, A., Wyld, M., and Burnstock, A. 1989. The Restoration of the Leonardo Cartoon. *National Gallery Technical Bulletin* **13**, 4-27

Harding, E. and Oddy, A. 1992. Leonardo da Vinci's Cartoon The Virgin and Child with St Anne and St John the Baptist. in *The Art of the Conservator* (ed. A. Oddy), 28-41. British Museum, London

Haskell, F. and Penny, N. 1981. *Taste and the Antique.* Newhaven

Hecquet, R. 1751. *Catalogue des Estampes Gravees d'apres Rubens ... Avec un Secret pour Blanchir les Estampes & en oter les taches d'huile.* Paris

IIC-Canadian Group, 1989. The Canadian Association of Professional Conservators 1989: *Code of Ethics and Guidance of Practice for those involved in the Conservation of Cultural Property in Canada* (2nd ed.)

IPC, 1991. *Code of Ethics and Professional Standards.* unpublished, distributed to members

Logan, H. (ed.) 1951. *How Much Do You Know About Glass?* New York

Mayor, A.H. 1980. *Prints and People: a Social History of Printed Pictures.* (2nd ed.) Princeton

Parshall, P.H. 1982. The Print Collection of Ferdinand Archduke of Tyrol. *Jahrbuch der Kunsthist. Sammlungen in Wien,* **LXXVIII,** 139ff

Priestly, J. 1770. *A Familiar Introduction to the Theory and Practice of Perspective.* London

Robison, A. 1977. *Paper in Prints.* National Gallery of Art, Washington

Ruskin, J. 1880. *Arrows of the Chace.* Vol.1, Orpington

Russell, H.J. and Abney, W. 1888. *Report ... on the Action of Light on Water Colours.* London

Rymaszewski, B. 1992. *Klucze Ochrony Zabytków w Polsce.* Warsaw

Sciola, G.C. (ed.) 1992. *Drawing, the Great Collectors.* Turin

Scott, A. 1921. *The Cleaning and Restoration of Museum Exhibits; Report upon Investigations conducted at the British Museum.* London

Scott, B. 1973. Pierre-Jean Mariette, Scholar and Connoisseur. *Apollo* **1,** 54-9

Slater, J.H. 1897. *Engravings and their Value.* (2nd ed.) London

Smith, R.D. 1987. Reversibility: A Questionable Philosophy. in *AIC Preprints,* 15th Annual Meeting Vancouver, British Columbia, Canada, 132-7

Stevenson, M. 1990. A Seventeenth Century Manual for the Restoration of Prints. *Print Quarterly* **VII,** 420-4

Taschini, P. 1943. *Domenico Grimani, Cardinale di San Marco.* Rome

Tuer, A.W. 1882. *Bartolozzi and his Works.* London

Viollet-le-Duc, E. 1875. *On Restoration.* London

IS WALL-PAINTING RESTORATION A REPRESENTATION OF THE ORIGINAL OR A REFLECTION OF CONTEMPORARY FASHION: AN AUSTRIAN PERSPECTIVE?

Heinz Leitner* and Stephen Paine**
*Hauptstrasse 3, 8742 Obdach, Austria
**66, Bradmore Park Road, London, W6 0DT

Perhaps more than any other works of art, wall-paintings intimately relate to their architectural context; the structure of a building acts simultaneously as the physical support and aesthetic setting for the painting. It is this fundamental relationship, between the painting and its surroundings, that exposes many of the problems associated with their restoration. Wall-paintings may not only signify art historical value, but also function emblematically within a religious or secular context. The didactic quality of wall-paintings may also reflect historic changes in taste and fashion - expressed through overpainted alteration or obliteration of the original image. The fifteenth-century exterior paintings at Ranten (in the region of Styria, Austria), for example, were altered in the late sixteenth century by the inclusion of a different colour scheme for the figure's halos, from ochre to azurite, as an attempt to unify the scheme with a new adjacent cycle of Protestant painting.

The relationship between the painting and its context, has been generated over the lifetime of the structure - a conglomerate of architectural and historic events and processes of decay, that must be contended with during any programme of restoration. Such interventions risk blurring boundaries and falsifying the relationship between a reflection of condition and the aesthetic appearance of the work of art. The proportion of balance between these two parameters rests with the subjective attitude and value judgements of a range of disciplines, that include conservators, conservation scientists, art historians, architects and clients.

THE HISTORIC BACKGROUND OF RESTORATION

The complex issues that today confront the restoration and conservation of wall-paintings, are historically only a relatively recent phenomenon. From the mid-nineteenth century onwards, the response by such activists as John Ruskin and William Morris to the destructive nature of much Victorian building restoration, initiated concerns for architectural preservation. This movement promoted the notion of historic buildings and their contents as important cultural and historic artefacts, worthy of preservation. William Morris, writing in 1877, justified the veracity of organically developed building renovations of the past against, as he saw it, the destructive nature of contemporary restoration, by stating that: 'if repairs were needed, if ambition or piety pricked on to change, that change was of necessity wrought in the unmistakable fashion of the time; a church of the eleventh century might be added to or altered in the twelfth, thirteenth, fourteenth, fifteenth, sixteenth, or even the seventeenth and eighteenth centuries; but every change, whatever history it destroyed, left history in the gap, and was alive with the spirit of the deeds done midst its fashion.' (Harvey 1972)

In contrast, the perception held of contemporary nineteenth-century restorations, is fittingly described by the Committee of the Society of Antiquaries (1855):

> The committee strongly urge that, except where restoration is called for in churches by the requirements of Divine Service, or in other cases of manifest public utility, no restoration should ever be attempted, otherwise than as the word 'restoration' may be understood in the sense of preservation from further injuries by time or negligence: they contend that anything beyond this is

untrue in art, unjustifiable in taste, destructive in practise, and wholly opposed to the judgement of the best archaeologists. (Cook and Wedderburn 1903-12, 245)

Morris and Ruskin were effectively demanding a cessation of the hitherto organic evolution of buildings, to be replaced with valued judgements about what should be preserved from the past: 'If it be asked us to specify what kind of amount of art, style, or other interests in a building, makes it worth protecting, we answer, anything which can be looked on as artistic, picturesque, historical, antique, or substantial: any work, in short, over which educated, artistic people would think it worthwhile to argue at all.' (Cook and Wedderburn, 1903-12, 212)

In principle at least, this thinking has, since the nineteenth century, been broadly held by the European approach to the preservation of historical and cultural artefacts[1]. An inevitable consequence, implicit in Morris' statement, is that subjective judgements are now inevitably required to ascertain the relative aesthetic, cultural and historic worth of individual works of art. The result of the increasing secularisation in the appreciation of historic works of art has largely seen the formal and historical qualities promoted over and above its original function.

APPROACHES TO RESTORATION

The status afforded works of art by such applied historicism sets the context for the many problems that are involved in the conservation and restoration of paintings. A polarisation in approaches to the treatment of wall-paintings is an inevitable outcome when dealing on the one hand with works of art, and on the other, a surviving historic document. The dichotomy facing the restoration of wall-paintings can, in principle, be divided between that of 'conserve as found' and 'restore to original'. The former approach effectively obviates the need to assign value judgements to any aspect of the appearance of the painting, other than attending to the stabilisation of the structural properties of the work. This approach can cause a dilemma when faced with a wall-painting scheme that has been overpainted and is now requiring treatment. For instance, the twelfth-century paintings in the charnel house at Hartberg (in the region of Styria, Austria), when discovered in the nineteenth century by Theophil Melicher (an artist working in the restoration of wall-paintings), were completely reconstructed by overpainting (Plate 1) (Anon 1892; Anon 1897; Graus 1902). Similarly, Romanesque paintings at Copford, Essex, had also been overpainted in the nineteenth-century style and perception of the Romanesque (Plate 2). The recent conservation approach to both schemes of painting has been to conserve as found and not to reveal the underlying original painting. While the temptation to recover the older and historically much rarer scheme may be strong, it can be argued however, that the later reconstructed image does still possess an historic veracity. By contrast, in Austria, medieval paintings in the chapel of St John (Pürgg, Styria) and the church of St Nicholas (Matrei), were both overpainted by nineteenth-century restorers. During the 1940s, these restorations were removed to reveal the original schemes, although the presentation of the paintings clearly demonstrates the subjective style of the restorers (Plate 3).

The term 'restore to original' is a misnomer, since the object can only effectively be returned to its original state as far as its present condition and architectural context allows - parameters subject to dramatic change over time. In this respect, wall-paintings differ fundamentally from easel paintings when the debate surrounding restoration pivots on 'aesthetic intention', and restoration itself focuses on levels of cleaning and surface retouching (Hedley 1985). Self-contained, portable, usually varnished and typically attributable to an aesthetic personality, easel paintings are susceptible to such an approach. But wall-paintings normally differ in all of these respects, imposing enormous and quite variable constraints on their treatment. Thus the debate regarding their restoration is no less vehement but less fully articulated.

Perhaps the most important aspect of painting is that it embodies within the brushstroke the hand of the artist - a sacrosanct element of artistic creativity. This is unlike architecture, where the creative process largely resides within the design rather than execution of this three-dimensional form and shape. While the replacement of worn masonry within a building does not necessarily damage the perception of the creativity of the architect, to overpaint damaged paint strokes fundamentally undermines our perception of a painting's ultimate artistic value. Thus, in wall-painting conservation, 'restoration', has come to mean, where and when it is deemed justifiable, re-establishing compositional values for areas of loss. This may take the form of neutral colour washes over areas of abrasion (*acqua sporca*), use of textured and toned plaster repairs, and the reconstruction (normally using non-deceptive techniques), of areas of loss where firm evidence obviates any conjecture, and which effectively re-establishes the compositional unity.

An example of this can be seen in the recent restoration of the fifteenth-century paintings by Masaccio, Masolino and Filippino Lippi in the Brancacci Chapel, Florence. The restorers recreated substantial passages of the painting based on an assessment of the reliability of quite substantial historic documentation (Baldini and Casazza 1992). A similar instance can be found in the Sistine Chapel. Restoration of Michelangelo's scene of *The Creation of Man* (possibly the most-recognised image of Renaissance art and the centrepiece of the chapel ceiling) extended, on the basis of known evidence, to the recreation of God's outstretched finger.

'Restore to original' may also involve the de-restoration of a painting. That is, the removal of retouchings from past interventions. In this instance photographs have proved a useful source in establishing a clearer idea of earlier, pre-restoration condition. For example, the current restoration of Leonardo's *Last Supper* has drawn upon the photographic record of Luigi Cavenaghi's 1904 restoration to verify alterations in figurative detailing introduced in 1954 by Mauro Pellicioli (Brambilla-Barcilon 1993).

CONSERVATION VERSUS RESTORATION

The treatment of wall-paintings comes under the broad headings of conservation and restoration. Conservation may be understood as technical intervention involved in the preservation of a wall-painting, where essential structural stabilisation theoretically does not, or at least is not intended to, alter the appearance of the painting. The visual image of wall-paintings, improved by certain forms of intervention, were formalised by Cesare Brandi in the 1960s (Brandi 1963). Two main elements of restoration can be considered: one, subtractive (cleaning); and the other, additive (treatment of surface lacunae and retouchings etc.).

The cleaning of a wall-painting can be important to its conservation, especially where harmful accretions are removed from the surface. Generally however, cleaning is a form of intervention that, while bringing enhanced clarity to the appearance of the painting, may also lead to the loss of historic covering layers and certain elements of the patination of the original paint layer.

The second intervention, involving material addition to the surface of the painting, is more likely to alter its appearance. Besides the multitude of different means available, this form of intervention is an inherently subjective one, that inevitably imparts a contemporary interpretation in its application.

A crucial difference in terms of reversibility divides these two aspects of restoration/conservation. Any material removed in the cleaning process can never be replaced. By contrast, however much material is added, assuming it to have been applied correctly, it can, in theory at least, be removed.

But such classification inevitably oversimplifies a complex situation. For example, cleaning may well be undertaken for conservation reasons but result in the dramatic alteration of the appearance

- the case of the Sistine Chapel becomes paradigmatic. The removal of later layers of glue that were pulling off Michelangelo's paint layer, resulted in an unprecedented 'restoration' of an image. In addition, various treatments of wall-paintings inevitably alter the image, most notably consolidation. Moreover, consolidation of a paint layer would not normally be undertaken without first cleaning. Thus the simplistic dichotomy between 'restoring' and 'conserving' becomes still less tenable. It is only when intervention extends beyond the bounds, literally the physical limits, of the surrounding original painting that the distinction becomes clear.

CONSTRAINTS ON TREATMENT

Significant constraints exist in the treatment of wall-paintings when compared with other works of art. Their scale, their technical problems, and their integral relationship to the structural context and its function, invariably draw together many other conservation disciplines - art history, architecture, conservation sciences, engineering etc. Moreover, the 'client' (the owner or agency responsible for the building) is not only unlikely to have any familiarity with conservation, either its technical or ethical aspects, but may have objectives which are in many instances, antithetical to the goals of conservation (Cather 1993). The work of all collaborating professionals comes under the broad range of ethical constraints that respect the physical, historic and aesthetic integrity of the object. These general principles include the reversibility of any treatment and restoration, that neither modifies nor conceals the authenticity of the object, and is distinguishable from the original (UKIC 1980; ICOMOS 1966).

Any restoration programme must inevitably respond to the demands not only of other professionals, but also to the expectations and objectives of the client. The type of painting (its aesthetic, cultural and historic importance), and its location can have a considerable impact upon the expectation of the final appearance of any painted scheme. The function of a building alone may determine how the restoration is carried-out.

In the late thirteenth-century church of St Lawrence (Styria), for example, numerous architectural changes and additions were made during various historic periods, leading to a variety of renovations to the architectural surfaces, through overpainting, whitewashing, and other decoration (Plate 4). Wall surfaces displayed a complex array of up to twenty different layers dating from the thirteenth to the twentieth century. A programme of uncovering and reintegration was carried-out between 1989-90. By exposing the earlier schemes of painting, a completely new and artificial 'moment' in history has been created (Dieplinger 1992)[2]. This form of intervention cannot be considered as conservation *per se*. The decision to uncover earlier layers of painting, subjectively construed to be of greater value, was made by the client and conservator, taking account of the function of the building. To avoid a potentially jarring juxtaposition between the uncovered medieval painting and the significantly more modern surrounding, treatment to both areas was considered necessary. This took the form not only of an aesthetic intervention to the paintings themselves, but also the reconstruction of surrounding architectural elements. By rooting the paintings within a more coherent and historically rational space, some of the aesthetic obstacles associated with such a complex situation are reduced. The form of intervention taken here is, however, only one of a range of possibilities available; others might include leaving the wall surface with the most recent *c*.1950 scheme; uncovering 'windows' displaying each phase in the evolving cycle of historic decoration; or, indeed, selecting a different period of painted decoration altogether for complete uncovering. The criteria for selection may take many forms. For instance, the highly deteriorated eighteenth-century painted decoration that obscured a fine medieval polychromy sculpture scheme on the exterior of the south portico of La Majestad de la Colegiata de Santa Maria La Mayor in Toro, Spain, was removed (1989-92) to reveal the earlier painting. The basis on which this decision was taken was that in Spain eighteenth-century painted sculpture remains reasonably common, while surviving medieval polychromy is extremely rare.

CASE STUDIES

To demonstrate the differing approaches and intervention decisions that can be taken when considering the conservation of wall-paintings, two specific examples from Austria will be discussed; the thirteenth-century paintings at the church of St George, Judenburg, and the sixteenth-century scheme in the Archbishop's Palace, Salzburg. Each location offers a wide variation both in terms of age, condition and function. Since both examples have only recently been uncovered, the problems associated with previous restorations do not arise. Both projects, however, are principally involved with the consequences imposed upon their conservation and presentation as a result of their location and uncovering.

The Church of St George, Judenburg

In 1987 a cycle of medieval wall-paintings, depicting the life of St George (c.1240), was discovered in this church (Brunner 1989; Lanc 1989). The decoration is in a domed space beneath the main tower, located between the fifteenth-century choir and the thirteenth-century nave (vaulted and enlarged in the seventeenth century) and typical of the Austrian medieval 'choir-tower-nave' church type. Since the space is relatively self-contained, it was decided to treat this area separately from other architectural surfaces in the building.

The recovery of this extensive scheme has been one of the highlights of recent wall-painting discoveries in the Austrian regions of Styria. In the centre of the dome is Christ surrounded by the four Evangelists, below are two tiers with Apostles, prophets and church fathers. Upon the walls is a cycle of the life of St George, set out in two registers of narrative. The radiating architectural elements painted within the dome reflect early Gothic rose-window design (Plate 5).

The excellent state of conservation of these paintings allowed careful study of the technique. They were found to have been executed in the *Kalkmalerei* (lime painting) technique, and not in true fresco. The ground is a roughly applied limewash, and the pigments - limited to red and yellow ochres and a substitute blue (made of carbon black and lime white) - were applied with lime and a small addition of an organic component (Leitner 1989). A characteristic of the painting style is the outlining of the figures with a fine black line.

The paintings were discovered during a routine investigation prior to redecoration. The decision to uncover these paintings was certainly taken on an archaeological and art historical basis, but also from the point of view of conservation, since large areas of the wall-paintings were being damaged by salt action beneath the covering limewash layers (Plate 6). The uncovering inevitably involved the destruction of historic limewash layers, and exposed the medieval painting to potential damage since it became the new interface between the ambient environment and the wall. But awareness of the full extent of the medieval scheme is important for its conservation since covered paintings are seriously at risk, particularly from, for example, misguided maintenance work to the fabric of the building.

The aesthetic presentation of the paintings could only be decided upon once the full extent and condition of the scheme had been revealed. It was found that the medieval paint layer contained a large number of varying sized surface losses, which by their contrasting lightness in tone to the original painting, significantly disrupted its legibility. These losses read as a dislocated layer in a plane in front of the painting. Two methods of reintegration were used. For small losses, *acqua sporca* (literally, dirty water, devoid of any colour value) was applied, while in larger losses, the effect of a corroded *arriccio* (base layer of plaster) was replicated in lime plaster fills, so that the losses would recede visually behind the plane of the image.

The effect of the *acqua sporca* is to reduce the dominance of the multitude of small losses, and to promote the original compositional coherence of the paintings. Reducing this particular visual disturbance allows the spectator to formulate a substantially more complete impression of the original.

Gallery of the Maps, Archbishop's Palace, Salzburg

The recent uncovering of the extensive sixteenth-century painted decoration in the Gallery of the Maps, (the *Landkartengalerie)* in the palace of the Archbishop, Salzburg, illustrates many of the problems introduced above (Wagner 1992; Schlegel 1992; Juffinger 1992a,b)[3]. This remarkable scheme was commissioned by Archbishop Wolf-Dietrich as part of his ambitious cultural and architectural renovation of Salzburg. Wolf-Dietrich (1587-1612), heavily influenced by the fashionable renaissance art in Italy where he spent much of his youth, presumably had central Italian models of 'map rooms' in mind (such as those in the Vatican, or in the Villa Farnese at Caprarola) when he commissioned his own *Landkartengalerie*, the only known example surviving north of the Alps.

The gallery connects two wings of the palace, is long and narrow (20m in length, 6m wide and 8m high), and was originally articulated by stucco pilasters, cornices and mouldings that framed paintings of townscapes in an upper register and corresponding maps of countries below (Plate 7). The room was radically altered during subsequent building renovations: the framing stucco was entirely removed; the painted walls were replastered and limewashed; the space was divided into a series of offices with lowered ceilings. The building as a whole has recently been subjected to a very thorough renovation and conversion programme to form the new Law Faculty of Salzburg University. It was during the initial phase of work to the fabric, that the paintings were discovered (Plate 8).

Pre-conservation analysis demonstrated a highly sophisticated technique. The pigments used included massicot, three organic colorants - indigo, cochineal (recently introduced from the New World) and Van Dyke brown (Cassel or Cologne earth, a bituminous material) - as well as the more familiar wall-painting colours of lead white, cinnabar, azurite, malachite, smalt, ultramarine, ochres and charcoal. The pigments were applied using egg as the binding medium, over a lime preparation layer that was found to contain casein with some animal glue. The base mortar (*intonaco*) revealed the presence of egg protein, probably applied as an initial sealant to the surface.

The decision to uncover was a particularly complex one in terms of conservation ethics. Initial tests proved highly damaging to the original paint layers. The final decision to proceed was made only on the basis of the development of a successful technique resulting from a two-year programme of experimentation. Having overcome the technical difficulties of the intervention, it was the historical importance of this rare scheme and its location in the heart of the culturally important city of Salzburg, that persuaded the client to proceed with a long-term and costly programme.

Following the uncovering - being greatly assisted by published copies of the original documentary sources for the maps and townscapes - the paintings were found to be in widely varying states of condition. These ranged from: surfaces completely intact displaying the full extent of the sophisticated painting technique; partially abraded areas; sections with only the underpainting and preparation layers; areas of complete loss of all painting; and finally to structural losses of the masonry support beneath. The variations can be accounted for by the diversity of renovation, in some areas involving scrapping down and limewashing of the paintings, in others hacking out of the stucco pilasters. The result was considerable visual confusion.

Attention to aspects of presentation has focused on a variety of aesthetic interventions, dependent upon the nature of the loss.

The large structural losses to the support that have occurred during the history of the room from, for example, previous inclusions of door openings and electrical conduits, were filled with masonry.

Areas originally unpainted and with deep losses were filled with an imitation version of the original *arriccio*.

Areas of painting where the *intonaco* is lost, were filled with a plaster mortar imitating the texture of the original *intonaco*. This material was also used to reconstruct missing edges and borders of the paintings. These techniques alone reinstated a significant level of compositional unity to the scheme.

For losses to the painting itself a variety of approaches were taken. The numerous small losses to much of the detailed information (place names, symbols and detailing of the towns, etc.) significantly hindered the legibility of these passages, so they were reintegrated using local colour. In limited areas of loss, where just the painted preparation layer survives, two approaches were taken: either neutral toning with *acqua sporca* mixed with a small percentage of local colour, or localised reconstruction, using the ground colour to re-establish greater coherence to the structure of the maps.

The non-figurative nature of the maps, when compared with, for example, the paintings at St George, Judenburg, does perhaps justify a slightly different approach to reintegration. Those small areas of reconstruction have been differentiated from the original through the use of a cross-hatched brush strokes. Since the paintings are direct and precise copies from a known published source - the townscapes are from Braun and Hoggenburg's *Civitates orbis terrarum* (published in six volumes between 1572 and 1617) and the maps from Ortelius' *Theatrum orbis terrarum* (published in 1570) - very accurate reconstruction to areas of loss was possible without resorting to conjecture (Plate 9).

The general ethos behind the decision to reintegrate the paintings was to achieve a balanced coherence between the quality and resonance of the original imagery and its post-uncovering condition. Following this stage of the presentation however, it became increasingly clear that the lack of the original stucco framing around the paintings adversely affected the overall aesthetic appearance of the gallery. Fortunately, enough crucial evidence survived of *in situ* preparatory sketches for the various elements of the architectural framing to allow a fairly clear idea of its original appearance. A variety of possibilities was considered as to how this important architectural dimension might be introduced. Total reconstruction was discounted, since certain areas of the design were unknown. It was also felt that a considerable ethical problem existed in terms of replacing as much as sixty percent of the wall surface with reconstructed stucco. The decision that has been taken will involve the reconstruction of the significant outlines of the stucco, without imitating any of the three-dimensional detailing. That this is a modern interpretation of the stucco decoration will be reinforced both in terms of the choice of contemporary material used and its means of application. Such a structure should inform the spectator of the major architectural dividing lines originally provided by the stucco decoration, as well as acting as a pictorial frame for the surviving paintings. The collaboration at this stage with a specialised architect was considered to be particularly important.

CONCLUSION

If restoration is to be seen only in the strict terms of the re-establishment of the original, and conservation only in terms of stabilising a situation as found, then a conflict between these parameters seems inevitable. What is required is a balanced approach that draws upon the combination of interpretations of the value of historical, as well as modern, surfaces as parts of a new *kunstwerk*. Combining aspects of restoration and conservation with critical scientific research and artistic understanding, will ensure that the work of art returns to its most significant legibility. That such an interpretation will be based on a contemporary fashion is unavoidable and inevitable. Yet, by the extension of decision-making across a broad-based range of disciplines, the specificity of subjective actions and the consequent risk to the preservation of an object, may be reduced.

ACKNOWLEDGEMENTS

The authors would particularly like to thank Sharon Cather, Conservation of Wall Paintings Department, Courtauld Institute, University of London, for her constant help and advice throughout the preparation of this paper.

NOTES

1. See International Charter for the Conservation and Restoration of Monuments and Sites, ICOMOS 1966. This document, drawn-up at the 2nd International Congress of Architects and Technicians of Historic Monuments (Venice 1964) attempted to qualify a firm definition of the guiding principles for the preservation and restoration of ancient buildings. The document reflects many of the ideas first expressed by Morris and Ruskin, when it states that 'imbued with a message from the past, the historic monuments of generations of people remain to the present day as living witnesses of their age-old traditions.

2. The painting scheme revealed in the nave, included ten rectangular panels with scenes from the life of Christ as well as a series of saints (Sts Erasmus, Catherine, Barbara and George), painted in the early-fifteenth century, and a Crucifixion and Last Judgement of the late-sixteenth century.

3. The Palace building is currently being restored to serve as the Law Faculty of Salzburg University, and the Gallery of Maps will be a reading room, forming part of the library complex. The conservation programme is headed by Heinz Leitner, under the authority of the Austrian Bundesdenkmalamt (Director, Dr Manfred Koller). The architect for the project is Paolo Martelotti (Rome). An international team of other research specialists are also involved. These include: Dr Mauro Matteini, Dr Arcangelo Moles, Sabino Giovanonni (Opificio delle Pietre Dure, Florence), Dr Hubert Paschinger (Laboratory of the Bundesdenkmalamt, Vienna) Dr Johannes Weber (Institut für technische Chemie, Akademie für angewandte Kunst, Vienna), Dr Duane Chartier, (ICCROM, Conserv Art Associates, Los Angeles) and Karol Bayer and Tatjana Bayer (Bratislava).

REFERENCES

Anon, 1892. Der Hartberger Karner und Seine Restauration. *Der Kirchenschmuck*, (Graz), **23**, 6

Anon, 1897. Romanische Malereien zu Hartberg. *Der Kirchenschmuck*, (Graz), **28**, 1-7

Baldini, U. and Casazza, O. 1992. *Brancacci Chapel Frescoes: Masaccio, Masolino, Filippino Lippi*. London

Brambilla-Barcilon, P. 1993. Etudes et Problèmes relatif à la Restauration de la Cène de Léonard da Vinci. in *Les Anciennes Restaurations en Peinture Mural*, 169-80. (Journal d'Etudes de la SFIIC, Dijon, 25-27 March 1993). Paris

Brandi, C. 1963. *Teoria del Restauro*. Rome

Brunner, W. 1989. Aus der Geschichte des Ortes und der Pfarrkirche. *Pfarrkirche St Georgen ob Judenburg*, 115-31. Graz

Cather, S. 1993. Conservation Principles and Practises: Complexity and Communication. in *Conservation of Ancient Sites on the Silk Road*, 39-44. (International Conference on the Conservation of Grotto Sites held at Mogao Grottoes, Dunhuang, China, October 3-8, 1993). Los Angeles

Cook, E.T. and Wedderburn, A. 1903-12. *The Complete Works of John Ruskin*, (39 vols.), Vol 8. London

Dieplinger, I. 1992. *The Church of St Lawrence, Styria*, 18-25, 61 ff. unpublished Diploma Thesis, Graz

Graus, J. 1902. Romanisch und Wandmalereien zu Pürgg und Hartberg. *Mitteilingen der K K Central-Commission für Erforschung und Erhaltung der Kunst- und Historischen Denkmale*, Vienna, **28**, 82

Harvey, J. 1972. *Conservation of Buildings*, Appendix III: The Manifesto of William Morris, 'Setting forth the Principles of the Society for the Protection of Ancient Buildings upon its foundation in 1877', 210-12. London

Hedley, G. 1985. On Humanism, Aesthetics and the Cleaning of Paintings. Two lectures to the Canadian Conservation Institute, February 1985, in *Measured Opinions: the collected papers on the Conservation of Paintings* (ed. C. Villers), 152-66. IIC, London

ICOMOS, 1966. *International Charter for the Conservation and Restoration of Monuments and Sites*. (2nd International Congress of Architects and Technicians of Historic Monuments). Venice

Juffinger, R. 1992a. Wolf Dietrich von Raitenau. *Katalog der Salzburger Landesausstellung*. Salzburg

Juffinger, R. 1992b. Die Galerie der Landkarten in der Salzburger Residenz, *Barockberichte*, **5 und 6**, 164-7

Lanc, E. 1989. Die spätromanischen Wandmalereien. *Pfarrkirche St Georgen ob Judenburg*, 47-96. Graz

Leitner, H. 1989. Berich über die Restaurierung. *Pfarrkirche St Georgen ob Judenburg*, 109-12. Graz

Leitner, H. 1992. Restauriebericht zu den Wanbildern der Landkartengalerie der Residenz. *Barockberichte*, **5 and 6**, 168-70

Schlegel, W. 1992. Zur Baugeschichte der Salzburger Residenz. *Barockberichte* **5 und 6**, 157-63

UKIC, 1980. *Guidance for Conservation Practice*. London

Wagner, F. 1992. Die Salzburger Residenz als Gegenstand Kunstgeschichtlicher Forschung, *Barockberichte*, **5 und 6**, 149-55

Plate 1   Hartberg (Styria)   Scene from an *Apocalypse* cycle before restoration

Plate 2   St.Mary (Copford, Essex).   *Christ in Majesty* (vault of the east apse).   The extensive Victorian reconstruction (1872, by Daniel Bell) of the original medieval scheme was, like Hartberg, conserved (1990 onwards).

Plate 3   St John (Pürgg, Styria). During the 1940s nineteenth-century overpainting was removed to reveal the original medieval scheme. The presentation then carried out, of the uncovered scheme, shows the delineation of form described in the repairs, and other retouching to losses.

Plate 4   St Lawrence (Styria). The removal of later covering layers have revealed a complex array of different historic features applied to the original fourteenth-century structure (fifteenth-century wall paintings, sixteenth-century vaulting and eighteenth-century pulpit). Such a situation presents considerable problems in terms of a valid historic presentation.

Plate 5   St George (Judenburg).   The ceiling decoration (*c.* 1240) of *Christ in Majesty*, after uncovering and reintegration of losses, following its discovery in 1987

Plate 6   St George (Judenburg).   Detail of the *Life of St George* cycle that extends around the walls below the ceiling paintings (after uncovering)

Plate 7 Archbishop's Palace, Gallery of Maps (Salzburg). A reconstructed model of the original appearance of the *Landkartengalerie* (*c.*1590).

Plate 8 Archbishop's Palace, Gallery of Maps (Salzburg): uncovering the paintings (1992)

Plate 9 Archbishop's Palace, Gallery of Maps (Salzburg). An example of (a) after uncovering and (b) the final presentation of one of the townscapes - *London*. The close correlation between the paintings and the original source (Braun and Hoggenburg's *Civitates orbis terrarum*), has allowed those few areas of loss to be accurately reintegrated.

CONSERVATION AND RESTORATION OF MINIATURES: PAST AND PRESENT

L.E. Fleming

Department of Conservation, The British Museum, London WC1B 3DG

INTRODUCTION

Miniatures were painted as illustrations to manuscript books in artists' studios which emerged during the fourteenth century in the scriptoria of the princely courts of India and Persia (Titley 1983). They were usually painted on paper made of flax fibre, sized with albumen or starch, and burnished with jade, glass or stone (Canby 1993). The artists of the early miniatures were Chinese, Persians, Mesopotamians, Mongols and Christians who influenced the style of the miniatures (Titley 1983). It appears that artists specialised in different aspects of the composition, such as producing the initial sketch, drawing portraits and faces, or incolouring. The composition would be sketched out in pencil or pounced through pin holes with charcoal from a preparatory design. This was then re-sized before painting. Some of the brushes were extremely fine and made of hairs of squirrels' tail or white Persian cats (Canby 1993). The materials used were usually of the highest quality, including lapis lazuli (natural ultramarine) and gold. Verdigris (basic copper acetate) and lead pigments were also widely used.

Paintings were often set on to a backing of four to five papers, and had coloured ruled lines drawn round them. Narrow paper borders were pasted round the edges before the paintings were set into an album leaf.

Initially the miniature paintings were incorporated onto the pages to make a design which was integral with the calligraphy (Plate 1), but eventually they were painted on a whole page, with margins which could be a plain colour, speckled with gold, or stencilled and hand coloured. For the most sumptuous manuscripts, the borders could also be elaborate works of art in their own right, such as floral and animal designs painted in as many as four shades of gold. Sometimes miniatures were also painted back to back on the same sheet, or they could be mounted back to back with several layers of paper between them. These methods of presentation can be the cause of physical damage.

DETERIORATION AND CONSERVATION

There are seven main causes of deterioration.

1. The various layers of backing papers and borders expand and contract by different amounts with changes in the relative humidity of the environment. This can cause: (i) cockling of the painted miniature giving rise to high points on which attrition can cause pigment loss; (ii) creasing and cracking of the paper carrying the image; and (iii) cracking and loss of flakes of pigment, or fine powdering of pigment on the convex or concave areas of cockling. When the pigment layer is particularly thick it is more likely to flake off, whereas thin, dry layers of pigment go powdery.
2. Careless handling which leads to tears and even to paper loss.
3. Insect pests, rats, and mice which will eat paper.
4. The use of verdigris (basic copper acetate) pigment which causes loss of paper due to the chemical action of the hydrolysis products of the pigment. Initially the affected paper turns

brown (just as it would when touched by a flame) (Plate 2), and eventually there is a total loss of the area covered by the green pigment.

5. Moisture and mould which stains the paper.
6. Silver paint, which subsequently becomes tarnished, was often used to depict water. Unfortunately there is no known treatment as yet.
7. The blackening of red and white lead pigments caused by environmental pollution. Hydrogen sulphide in the air turns white lead carbonate into black lead sulphide.

It is possible for a conservator to repair most types of damage mentioned above. The cockling sometimes presents a problem if two paintings are mounted back to back on the same paper supports or painted on the same sheet of paper, but if the painting can be separated from its borders and backing sheets then it can usually be flattened.

The movement of the miniature support, the linings, the borders, and the album leaf creates tensions in all the different papers. General cockling as well as creasing across the corners of the miniature was treated in the past by the addition of more layers to the decorative borders. These would again move at a different rate when the relative humidity of the atmosphere changed, thus exacerbating the problem. The end result was often borders which were too small for the miniature. The most successful way to solve that problem today is to separate the miniature from its backings and borders, flatten it and re-assemble it with only one border in the album leaf, if necessary adding extra pieces to the borders to accommodate the size of the miniature. If there are several layers of borders, every effort should be made to preserve them during dismantling so that they can be kept separately in the same mount after conservation.

Attrition of the high points and loss of pigment because of the movement of the paper may leave the paper support exposed. In the past these small areas have sometimes been painted in. The results are rarely successful. Apart from the ethical considerations, the colours often do not match exactly. New pigments do not age and discolour at the same rate as the original ones and, more importantly, the artistic ability of the conservator is unlikely to match the skill of the original artist.

Even when relatively large areas of the miniatures are missing attempts have sometimes been made in the past at restoring the image, usually with disastrous results. These restored areas were painted directly on to the original support paper and cannot now be removed, thus spoiling several very beautiful works of art (Plate 3).

In contrast to these earlier approaches to restoration, the modern conservator takes a minimalist approach. As far as missing pigment is concerned, it is not replaced, but surrounding areas where the pigment is still present but in danger of being lost because it is powdering or flaking, should be consolidated. Lacunae and larger missing areas can be filled with a suitable matching paper using gluten-free wheat-starch paste.

The most important treatment of the degradation of paper caused by verdigris is to de-acidify it to prevent further deterioration. Magnesium bicarbonate in Klucel G (hydroxyl-propyl-cellulose) can be brushed on locally (Banik *et al.* 1982). As well as deacidifying the area, this has the advantage of encapsulating the pigment granules and helping to separate them from the paper fibres, thus reducing the potential of the verdigris to cause further damage.

There is, however, very little to be done about moisture and mould stains as many of the paints usually used for the miniature are fugitive in water and any conservation which involves bleaching or aqueous treatments cannot be used.

When conservation is complete, the question of restoration must be considered.

DISCUSSION OF THE ETHICS OF RESTORATION OF PAINTED MINIATURES

One of the basic ethical considerations for paper conservation is that it should be reversible, hence inpainting on the original paper, which is obviously not reversible, is unacceptable. Secondly, the artists producing these miniatures were of the highest virtuosity who used paints made in their studios, usually of the best materials. For these reasons, the British Museum has decided to leave areas where there is pigment loss and no other damage, without any further interference.

The British Museum approach to restoration recognises the importance for scholars who examine the miniature closely of being able to see the condition of the original painting as it is today. That is part of its history.

Where there is paper loss, it can be replaced or filled in. The repair paper is toned to match the colour of the paper carrying the image. When the painting is on exhibition the eye accepts the missing area. Even if the repair is reversible (i.e. removable), the missing image should not be completed. Hiding repairs and missing areas by overpainting conceals the history of the object. To preserve the integrity of the miniature, repairs must be visible on close examination. One miniature which shows the impossibility of doing anything other than toning to a background colour because of the complexity of the image is that depicting *Sir Thomas Roe at the Court of Jāhangir* of *c*.1620 (Plate 4). However, this is not always so. For example, in some cases where the verdigris used to paint leaves has caused loss of the paper, it could be tempting to restore the infills to a green colour. The temptation should be resisted.

The colour of the paper carrying the image varies with each miniature. The repair paper can be coloured with watercolours to match exactly. An even tone is usually achieved by immersing or spraying the repair paper before using it. The repairs then blend in with the original background and are totally acceptable, while still showing the true condition of the painting.

The *Thomas Roe* miniature depicts an important historical event. Another painting of historical importance is *The Princes of the House of Timur* of *c*.1550. This was altered when the rulers of the time changed (Rogers 1993) and research has shown that only five figures are totally original. Faces were altered during Jāhangir's reign (between 1605 and 1620) and one figure has been totally removed to be replaced by another. It is thought that some figures were added later still. These alterations were done by the leading artists of the time, are signed, and have to be accepted as part of the composition as they were ordered by the ruler of the day. There is a tradition among easel paintings 'restorers' which involves the removal of later overpainting to return the painting to its original state. Often this reveals more in the composition than was evident. In general the materials used in miniatures (i.e water-based pigments on paper) preclude the removal of any later painting. Later additions to miniatures were just that, additions not eliminations, so that the removal of later additional painting, if it were possible, would result in empty spaces. The subject of the *Princes of the House of Timur* is dynastic, and the figures are named. They were added in a historical context, and the painting would be reduced in value to scholars without its additional figures. Unfortunately large areas of the painting are missing, some due to the action of verdigris, and they will be replaced in a neutral tone.

Whether the Persian miniature of *A Prince and page riding on an elephant*, painted in the sixteenth century, is enhanced by the overpainting is questionable. It seems to have travelled to Turkey and got damaged quite early in its existence (Plate 5). There are two major tears and damage along the bottom edge which is possibly caused by verdigris. These areas have been overpainted with trees and flowers in the Turkish style, probably in the seventeenth century, and it is possible that the ultramarine of the canopy was also added at that time. This early restoration is preserved for ethical and historical reasons, although the impossibility of removing the overpainting without ruining the original had to be considered. It is always of interest to the art historian, as well as to the conservator, to have access to early repairs and restoration, provided they are not causing additional damage, as, for example, some adhesives do. While it is detective work to discover the history of the 'life' of this painting, it is reassuring to know that today all changes caused by conservation are carefully recorded. Furthermore, inpainting or overpainting is not an example to be followed.

The one exception to this rule of no coloured inpainting is the repair of plain borders. As the repairs of the borders do not interfere with the miniature itself, it has been decided by British Museum curators that the repairs to the borders can be toned to the same colour as the original, usually red or brown. This treatment seems to draw the miniature together as a cohesive whole. Naturally this does not apply to elaborate decorative borders.

One miniature carrying old repairs is *Prince Khurran weighed in gold and silver* of *c*.1615. The previous repairs were done using gold paper. There is so much gold paint in the miniature, however, that the gold paper repairs do 'disappear' in all the glitter. They have been left *in situ* in spite of not quite fitting the usual ethical criteria. In this case it would be possible to remove the old repairs, but historical interest in early conservation methods prevents this, as they do not appear to be causing additional damage.

What is to be done about the blackened lead pigments? The molecular layer which has turned into black lead sulphide can be converted into white lead sulphate which will not turn black again. This is not the same substance which the artist used, but it is the same colour. It is certain that the artist did not intend the white, orange, pink or light blue colours on the miniature to be a greyish black. This can justifiably be called restoration, and in this instance it is a treatment which should be seriously considered.

CONCLUSION

For Oriental miniatures the toning of repairs has to be treated with the greatest discretion. Paper conservation is generally guided by rules which originated when the principles of archive repair were drawn up by Roger Ellis (Ellis 1951). He included three fundamental rules:

1.   As far as possible, to replace missing material with new material of the same kind;
2.   To leave the nature and extent of the repair unmistakably evident;
3.   Never to do anything which cannot be undone without damage to the original.

Even the wording of these principles include an escape route, by writing 'as far as possible' Ellis left room for uncertainty. The discussions of several case histories above show that, in fact, no definite rules can be laid down. The repair paper is toned, the solid border repairs are coloured to match the original, and blackened lead pigments can be converted to their original splendour. Each case is unique and must be considered individually. But the one principle which is absolutely certain is that, these days, inpainting on the original is totally unacceptable.

The conservators aim should be to:

1.   repair the work of art and prevent further deterioration;
2.   preserve the integrity of the object;
3.   reveal the history of the object;
4.   make it acceptable for exhibition.

There is always the temptation to make a work of art look 'as good as new'. It may be satisfactory for the conservator; it appears to demonstrate skill to the layman; but the discipline of restraint tempered by knowledge is preferable.

REFERENCES

Banik, G., Stachelberger, H., and Wächter, O. 1982. Investigation of the Destructive Action of Copper pigments on Paper and Consequences for Conservation. in *Science and Technology in the Service of Conservation* (N.S. Bromelle and G. Thomson eds.), 75-8. IIC, London

Canby, S.R. 1993. *Persian Painting*. London

Ellis, R. 1951. *The Principles of Archive Repair*. London College of Printing, London

Rogers, J.M. 1993. *Mughal Miniatures*. London

Titley, N.M. 1983. *Persian Miniature Painting*. London

Plate 1   A miniature set into a page of calligraphy: Bizhan and Farūd in single combat from the Epic *Shahnama of Firdausi* (22 x 15cm; 1948,10-9,050)

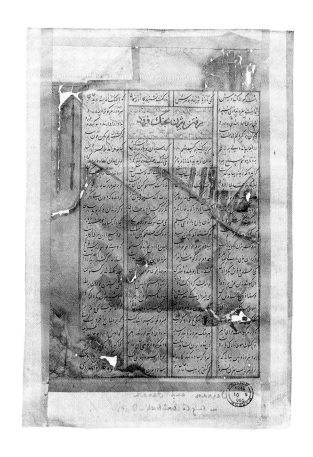

Plate 2   Verso of Plate 1 in transmitted light, showing 'burnt' areas and paper loss caused by the use of verdigris pigment on the recto   (22 x 15cm; 1948,10-9,050)

Plate 4   Sir Thomas Roe at the court of Jahangir showing repair of paper loss along the right-hand
edge   (23.3 x 14.3cm; 1933,6-10,01)

Plate 3 Detail of the animals assembled to complain to the raven, showing old restoration in the top left-hand corner (1920,9-17,05)

Plate 5   A prince and page on an elephant. The trees and floral foreground are overpainted to hide previous damage. (25 x 18.7cm; 1937,07-10,0328)

RESTORATION: ACCEPTABLE TO WHOM?

Tiamat Molina and Marie Pincemin
Atelier Régional de Restauration, Château de Kerguehennec, 5600 Bignan, France

INTRODUCTION

Brittany has a particularly rich heritage in the field of statuary; today more than 3,500 sculptures in Brittany are protected, preserved within museum collections or classified as 'Historic Monuments'. As the majority have religious origins they also form part of a living heritage and are used during festivals or in daily worship. Around 80% are preserved *in situ*, in churches and chapels.

It is in this context that, at the instigation of a group of museum curators (BUHEZ-VIE), the Atelier Régional de Restauration was created. Registered by the Ministry of Culture (Directions des Musées de France et des Monuments Historiques), its job is the preservation of the region's polychrome sculptures. Answering to local needs and requirements, its advice is sought by a wide variety of people: both professional (museum curators, Historic Monument inspectors, etc.) and non-professional (mayors, priests, heads of associations, etc.). This results in a wide range of requests and perspectives for intervention.

SOME EXAMPLES

In general, the preservative treatments undertaken are well understood and accepted. They aim to stabilise the object in its current state, whilst making few visual modifications.

The restoration treatments themselves often cause significant aesthetic changes (the reconstruction of forms, retouching of colours) which may give rise to discussion, debate and controversy. Who, then, determines the limits of intervention? Is it the restorer who should decide upon the framework for his work? Is it the person responsible for the administration of the object? Is it the perspective as seen by the user which directs the intervention and so decides the outcome? Can one person alone determine the limits of each restoration?

Specific examples will be used to demonstrate the questioning and hesitations, as well as the evolution of daily practices which more and more integrate consultation with dialogue.

A. A piece of restoration refused

Saint André, the chapel of Locjean, commune of Rosporden (Finistère)
Polychrome statue in wood, nineteenth century (?). Ht. 180cm; Length 100cm; Depth 28cm

This item, kept in a chapel, was entrusted to the Atelier with a request for preservation. It displayed, in particular, signs of having been attacked by parasites in earlier times, leading to the extremities of the cross crumbling away. The work was carried out without our deeming it necessary to fill in the missing parts, which were small and hardly visible. The administrator responsible for this object, the Conservateur des Antiquités et Objets d'Art, who was consulted when the work was finished, gave his approval to the treatment carried out.

Saint André was therefore put back into the chapel and, on this occasion, the conserved statue was presented to the members of the association for the preservation of the site. Their reaction was quick to come: why had the missing parts not been filled in? Or, even more simply, why had the cross-piece of the cross not been replaced with new wood? Was the Atelier incapable of such a simple piece of work? A sculpture which has been 'restored' must be complete. The programme of conservation was, therefore, unacceptable. Despite explanations, the Atelier could make no further progress and the work had to be redone.

B. An unbalanced restoration

Saint Candide, commune of Scaer (Finistère)
Polychrome statue in wood, nineteenth century(?) (Plate 1) Ht. 147cm; Length 50cm; Depth 45cm

This statue, whose neo-gothic polychromy was particularly incomplete, is of great historical interest to the commune, whose parish church bears the name of Sainte Candide.

The request was for a complete restoration so that it might be returned to its place in church services. Due to budgetary limitations, after a preservative treatment to the entire piece, a coloured reintegration was performed, with particular regard to the face but less detailed on the remainder. In this way, the face was restored by more than 50% with the aim of giving new life to the statue.

The finished article satisfied both the Conservateur des Antiquitiés et Objets d'Art and the parishioners, but poses several questions to the restorer. What determining factors should direct the work: the function of the object, the budget available or the beauty of the sculpture? To what extent should the function of the object count in the direction of the restoration? Can one treat items from museums in a different way to religious items?

C. Restoration accepted then reworked

Saint Apolline and her executioners, Musée Départemental Breton, Quimper (Finistère)
Polychrome statue in oak, second half of the fifteenth century (Plate 2) Ht. 160cm; Length 80cm; Depth 25cm

This group, preserved in a museum, represents the martyrdom of Saint Apolline. The Saint and one of the executioners are carved from the same block of wood, the other executioner being made from a separate block. Both blocks had been badly attacked by parasites; the damage caused leading to a lack of stability. The lone executioner, in particular, needed to be restabilised, and this was done by the addition of a minimum of material accompanied by a coloured reintegration. This intervention was purposely limited and carefully carried out, the blocks imitating the damaged wood were put into place. An interview took place with a member of the museum curatorial team in order to present the work which had been carried out and this lead to an agreement regarding the choice of the type of restoration, with which we are here concerned, that of stabilisation.

Once returned to the collection, the statue became the subject of a new presentation made by the museum's technical team. When this new 'improvement' was inspected three months later, the conservators observed that its base had been entirely reworked and closed up with a plug (plaster, resin?) and tinted brown (paint?). Furthermore, a metal shaft had been added, fixed to the back of the statue by a screw.

These interventions display the lack of consultation within the museum itself and the poor understanding of the minimal repairwork of stabilisation; repairwork which could appear to have left the piece in a fragile condition.

D. Restoration of a group of statues: dialogue and evolution of the concept of the work completed

This ensemble, which comes from one chapel, comprises four statues from the sixteenth century and one from the seventeenth, which today form an homogenous group, regularly repainted. All display signs of having been badly attacked by parasites, resulting in large losses of material, the peeling off of colour and are, in general, clogged up with dirt. A uniform preservation treatment was carried out by the Atelier on these objects at the request of the Conservateur des Antiquités et Objets d'Art. The restoration treatment itself was individualised whilst, at the same time, keeping a unity of intervention. The curator was regularly consulted with regard to the possible treatments. During these consultations, the Atelier endeavoured to develop the idea of the finished article, particularly as regards the reconstruction of the forms and the colour retouching.

SAINT JACQUES (Plate 3)

This little statue which is of great aesthetic quality was the object of a thorough intervention. The foot of the statue was restored by the addition of a base in resin with reintegration of form and colour. In the same way, many folds in the drapery, the nose, and fingers were rebuilt and retouched.

PIETA

The treatment consisted of an almost total reconstruction, both in form and colour for certain sections (the nose and the belly of Christ, the folds in the drapery) but there are still signs of wear and tear in the least visible sections (the top of the Virgin's head, certain folds in the drapery).

SAINT HERBOT

The forms were almost totally reconstructed, although the colours were on the whole left untouched.

SAINT EVÊQUE (Plate 4)

There was extensive reconstruction of the forms, particularly on the sides of the statue. The reintegration of colours being limited to the anterior face (front view), the rebuilding of the sides remaining in coloured woodpowder.

Moving from one item to another, dialogue enabled us to develop the ideal restoration required, to the point where it was possible to fill in gaps visible in the reconstruction of the forms.

E. Restoration misunderstood

This statue of Saint Evêque, part of the group presented above, had suffered a bad attack by parasites which had damaged the wood leading to many parts being lost, including the right hand, which very probably held a cross. By plugging and rebuilding the forms we were able to give the statue a certain unity. But the reconstruction of the hand and the cross had not been envisaged either by the curator or by the Atelier. Once the restoration was finished, and the statue set back in its accustomed place in the church of Bénodet, where it was welcomed with a Blessing, the parish priest expressed his astonishment at the lack of the cross, something which he felt indispensable if the statue was to be recognised for what it was.

The absence of any ancient documents which might have authorised the reconstruction of the cross did not appear to him to be sufficient argument not to return the statue to its religious function once more.

F. Incompatibility between requirements and practices

Sometimes intervention is refused when requirements are incompatible with normal restoration practices, for example, the complete repainting of an item or the reconstruction of elements which have disappeared and for which there are no local documents. The items are sometimes then entrusted to local craftsmen who, in order to comply with the request in every respect, carry out restoration which is harmful or actions which are destructive (stripping, repainting).

These practices are questionable. Would it be appropriate to ease the code of ethics, in order to avoid restorations which are both crude and destructive? Can a code of ethics which is adaptable to each situation or to each item be considered? What then would be the limitations?

ONE SOLUTION: DIALOGUE

These difficulties have led more and more to discussions with those responsible for the items and to those who use them. Systematic dialogue takes place around an object, or a group of objects, in the course of restoration in the workshop. But equally, wider dialogue with the general public to bring the details to their attention is essential.

A. Meeting around a single object

Meetings are now called systematically at key moments in the restoration process and, in particular, before retouching starts. These dialogues bring together at the Atelier curators of Antiquités et Objets d'Art, inspectors of Historic Monuments, museum curators, mayors, priests and heads of associations, all of whom are always interested in such exchanges, even if they do not see their usefulness beforehand. In this way, each interested party can specify their expectations, their constraints (practical, technical, financial), and can explain their orientation and their choice. Such meetings give rise to agreements which benefit the objects themselves. They enable them to receive the best restoration possible and render each person concerned responsible, so ensuring a satisfactory long-term conservation of our cultural heritage.

B. Meeting around a group of objects

The Atelier is directed more and more towards the conservation of not only single items but of groups in their original context: a collection already put together, the patrimony of a church, a commune, or a château. Here, the intervention is not only directed towards restoration, but equally offers advice, an assessment of the state of the items concerned, recommendations for conservation to be undertaken, directions that the treatment should follow, and the priorities.

AN EXISTING COLLECTION (ethnographical items belonging to the Societé Polymathique of Vannes)

A detailed examination of each item was carried out, leading to a written report on the state of preservation, treatments recommended in order of priority, and advice on presentation and storage.

THE PATRIMONY OF A CHÂTEAU (Museum of Rochefort-en-Terre, Morbihan)

All wooden items preserved in the château were examined: statues, furniture, picture frames. An assessment was made of each room giving a description of the state of the items and advice on their protection during the winter (the museum being open to the public only in the summer season).

THE PATRIMONY OF A CHURCH (Parish church, Landevennec, Finistère)

The report of an active attack by parasites on a statue, noticed by the local services, led to the Atelier being called in to intervene in this case only. Following our advice, all fourteen sculptures in the building, plus those in an adjoining chapel, were examined. A detailed fiche was drawn up for each item as well as an estimate of the cost of restoration for the most seriously damaged or the most interesting items. At the same time, the Atelier suggested spending two days working on the site. This would allow them to treat with insecticide *in situ*, with a team of local workers to help with the handling and dusting of each item.

The Atelier Régional does not have the means to share in the day to day upkeep of all the statues in Brittany. By working together in this way, it should be possible to avoid the most frequent mistakes: fractures resulting from clumsy handling, sudden changes in climatic conditions, etc. Such days also enable an inventory of the local patrimony (by photography and documentation) to be drawn up, and to keep the general public informed about the importance of preservation.

C. Meeting around the methods of restoration

In France every autumn, *Journées du Patrimoine* (Cultural Heritage Days) are held. For one week-end, both public and private establishments open their doors free of charge to the general public. For the last three years, the Atelier at Kerguehennec has taken part in this event. The premises are prepared to receive visitors. Working methods and products used are exhibited and sculptures shown in the different phases of treatment (consolidation, refixing, cleaning, retouching, examination, dossier). Explanatory panels are set up and visits carried out at regular intervals, led by the conservators themselves. In this way the true role of the conservators can be made known. At these times the Atelier receives between 500 and 900 visitors per day (church members, societies and craftsmen) who sometimes come back to ask for opinions and advice.

Training days have also been organised on the theme of the preservation of polychrome sculptures and textiles. Aimed at the technical staff of museums, members of societies for the protection of chapels and, indeed, anyone faced with the practical problems relating to the preservation of collections, their object was to teach how to look at works in the hope of preventing further decay. This initiative met with great success. Each 'day' was held at Kerguehennec, thus enabling a visit of the workshop to be made.

CONCLUSION

Discussions are carried out with many partners. Their approach to items under examination, their points of view, and their interests differ and are sometimes in opposition. The Atelier, the meeting point of their requests, sometimes finds itself in a difficult position.

Experience has shown that ignorance of restoration and its ethics was often the basis of refusals. It therefore seemed necessary to us to develop a variety of informative actions which could be integrated into our daily practices. This long-term task is one of the roles of the Atelier Régional. Essential to the conservation of our patrimony, it must help to make the current principles of restoration acceptable to all.

Plate 1   St Candide,   Commune of Scaër (Finistère)
Plate 2   St Apolline and her executioners, Musée Départmental Breton, Quimper (Finistère)

Plate 3   St Jacques,   Chapelle du Perguet, Benodet
Plate 4   St Evêque,   Chapelle du Perguet, Benodet

GILTWOOD RESTORATION - WHEN IS IT ACCEPTABLE?

Colin Jenner

The Wallace Collection, Hertford House, Manchester Square, London W1M 6BN

This paper is intended to discuss the issues surrounding the debate on the restoration of gilded wood within a museum context.

Gilding has been, for most of its history, at the mercy of its own richness. Its message of opulence and taste was never allowed to diminish, so when the gold grew a little sad through misuse or unfavourable environmental conditions, the object would be regilded (Considine 1989). Tastes changed as various colours of leaf, ground, varnish and different styles of application became fashionable. A new upholstery fabric could occasion the sprucing up of tired gilding on a chair. Prior to a gilded object being sold, there was (and still is, to a large extent) a very high probability that it would be regilded to entice a prospective purchaser by imparting a sense of newness to an old object. Gilding was treated in much the same way as a picture varnish, i.e. it could be replaced when it appeared to hinder appreciation of the object. Unfortunately this practice was, until recently, still common in museums.

It is worth making the point that a well-maintained object is less likely to need restoring. Water gilding can be one of the least durable finishes that there is and the environment in which an object is kept can shorten its expected life. If the air is dry for a long time the wood can shrink away from the gesso, causing the gesso to buckle and fall away. If the humidity is too high it can swell the wood and split the gilded surface, again potentially causing loss. High water content will re-swell the glue in the gesso, causing problems whilst being handled, as well as allowing mould to grow. Dust is often much thicker than the leaf itself and dusting will cause abrasion to the gold if there is no protective layer. Gilding should be treated with the utmost care and handling kept to a minimum (always with gloves).

How, then, does the situation arise where conservators even talk of restoration in a museum environment? One answer is obvious: even the best, most stable museum atmosphere can only postpone the inevitable deterioration of the organic materials that make up works of art with gilded finishes. There is another, more subtle, reason: conservators and restorers alter what they touch. Objects are rarely returned to the condition they were in immediately before the intervention started. How many conservators replace the dirt they have removed? To what time in the life of the object has the intervention 'returned' it? Cleaning is a process of restoration. Conservation would involve rendering accretions harmless by stabilising them and leaving them there. The aim of conservators is to attempt to arrest the actions of time, while preserving its effects.

A gilded chair, used regularly, will lose areas of finish on, for instance, the arms and the legs. This distressing differs from other types of wear only in the fact that it is the result of natural use and imparts a sense of history to an object. It is the reason behind the loss which is the determining factor in distinguishing these marks from unnatural wear. A conservator must be careful not to bring preconceptions to an object, as areas of loss on an unexpected part of the object may point to a part of its history as yet unlooked for. Distressed areas on opposing members of a picture frame may indicate that it was turned upside-down at some date and may lead to interesting conclusions that would have been missed had they been hidden by restoration.

Although the practice of conservation and restoration has been recognised for a long time, it is only in recent years that they have come to have different meanings (Corfield 1988). Conservation is preserving the work of art as it is at present. This is most effectively achieved (indeed, technically, can only be achieved) by passive or preventative conservation, such as controlling the environment and limiting the amount of handling of the object. Unfortunately the conditions that would arrest decay effectively (a dark room filled with inert gas) would not be comfortable for the visiting public! Restoration is usually taken to mean a process that will change the present appearance of an object by removing or adding material, usually to give the object an earlier historical perspective. However, at the Wallace Collection this definition can be slightly tempered due to the nature of the museum. Lady Wallace bequeathed part of her collection of works of art to the nation in 1897. The accepted reading of her will implies that the collection should stand as a testament to the Victorian founders as well as the patrons and artists of the works of art. Thus, it could be reasoned that in order to conserve the collection, we first need to restore the objects to the condition that they were in 1897. We would argue that restoring objects to their 1897 condition is conserving the collection in its broadest sense, as far as this is possible.

While few hard and fast rules on the ethics of restoration can be set, some points may be made. Any work is only carried out after a set of questions has been answered. These include: why is the object in need of attention and how should any proposed scheme be carried out? It is important to understand the real reasons why an object has been chosen for treatment, not least so that one may achieve the desired end result. Sometimes it is not the object at all which is the problem, but an external factor, such as unflattering light, or a strong wall colour affecting the colour of the gold. Changing the wall colour is more expensive than adding a tonal layer to the object, but it is the only course open to a conservator. Picture frames frequently have their finishes tampered with in order to do justice to the subtle tones of a canvas or panel, when the actual cause of the problem is the greater amount of ambient light in galleries today compared with the day that the frame was made.

The decision as to which object to bring to the workshop is rarely made solely on conservation grounds. It is the museum curator who usually decides, for aesthetic reasons, that an object should be worked on. Restoration of an object is often initiated through a feeling that the object cannot be properly understood, or that the missing area interferes with the interpretation offered to the viewer, or even simply because it is thought that the object could look better than it does at present. Objects in museums have often acquired an indefinable quality that only time can bestow. This is often the first casualty in any restoration and is, practically speaking, impossible to duplicate in any timespan or environment other than that which produced it in the first place.

Can the integrity of an object be compromised by showing only the original material, with all the bumps and losses that accompany an object with a history? If, for instance, the original scheme of a chair is unbalanced (and therefore unreadable) by large areas of the white ground showing through loss of the gilding, would it be advisable to regild the losses? Possibly the most desirable option would be to show a replica of the object in its original glory alongside the museum object in its present conserved state. This would satisfy both the purists, who may feel able to interpret all the signs of the object's history and therefore gain more from its unrestored condition, as well as the more casual visitor who wishes to 'see how we used to live' and would enjoy the more 'finished' piece. However, the prospect of having to double gallery space is not one that many museums can take seriously, although this solution can be used in exceptional instances to great effect. Where there is more than one identical object in a collection, an alternative solution would be to restore some and leave others untouched as study pieces. A thorough examination of the set is first needed in order to make the (possibly arbitrary) decision as to which to restore.

Once the decision to restore a gilded object has been made, it is still common practice to distress (i.e. rub off) the restored area. Gold infills need to match the surrounding finish but, if it has been decided to carry out a complete regilding, as sometimes happens, then there is no need to distress at all. Often the only way that original gilding can be identified is by reading the distressed areas and being convinced by them. If the new gold is distressed the restorer would actually be attempting to mislead people into believing that the gold is of some age and has been subjected to the rigours of normal use (which is not true). However, new gold is often toned in order to allow it to fit into its surroundings. If this is not done, it is likely that it will detract from other objects in the room. It may also be necessary to accentuate the depths of the carving with a toned medium, because due to the increase in lighting levels, the subtle variations of light and shade can disappear, resulting in a perceived loss of detail on the ornament.

There can be a tendency for more restoration to be carried out to a timescale of exhibitions than is proper for the welfare of objects. Rushed or incomplete restoration can compound problems for future conservators and can only serve to endanger the object. The time when objects are most at risk from harm is during the preparation for, and transportation to and from, exhibitions. There are critics who go so far as to call for a moratorium on the movement of works of art, for the 'rights of works of art'. From a conservation viewpoint there is much to be said for this; a large amount of restoration would be avoided if objects did not suffer from 'post traumatic exhibition syndrome'. Conservation should work to its own timetable, dictated by the condition of the works of art, and conservators must be careful not to allow the amount of restoration (as opposed to conservation) that they carry out to become the measure by which they are judged.

How to do the work is the question that conservators spend most time contemplating, and it is in this area that gilding is possibly lagging behind other areas of conservation. When removing over-gilding we should be aware of any glaze or size sandwiched between the layers. Knowledge of these coatings is vital in furthering the skill of presenting objects in the condition in which they should be seen. There can be no doubt that gilders used many different techniques to create subtle effects designed to enhance the appearance of gold (Cession 1990; Considine 1991). Some of the materials used were light fugitive, making them difficult to identify today, but traces will remain deep in the crevices. Any such coating should be replaced as part of a restoration.

Gilding is a finishing effect. The preparations that underlay the leaf can be non-traditional in order to differentiate them from original materials and make it easier to remove them without damaging the object (Thornton 1991). The standard technique of applying an isolation layer over the cleaned object before filling any losses achieves this. Traditional collagen sizes can be difficult to remove without damage to the gold and also tend to attract grime to the object. On areas that will not be visible, such as a base for infills or under missing ornament, a more viscous isolation solution can be used. Because these areas are out of sight there is little problem with the coating forming an interference layer of serious consequence. Where possible it is a good idea to mark areas of restoration so that they may be easily read using special equipment. Fluorescing pigments will be visible under ultraviolet light and the use of barium sulphate in a gesso mixture will make it opaque to x-rays.

Restoration will remain a contentious part of conservation work so long as conservators endeavour to balance the aesthetic qualities of works of art against their historical integrity.

BIBLIOGRAPHY

Cession, C. 1990. The surface layers of baroque gildings: examination, conservation, restoration. in *Cleaning, Retouching and Coatings* (J.S. Mills and P. Smith eds.), 33-5. IIC, London

Considine, B. 1991. Gilders art in eighteenth century France. in *Gilded Wood: Conservation and History* (ed. D. Bigelow *et al.*), 87-98. Madison, Connecticut

Considine, B. 1989. Damaged Giltwood: a change in ethics. *Apollo*, November 1989, 312-20

Corfield, M. 1988. Towards a conservation profession. in *Preprints for the UKIC 30th Anniversary Conference* (compiled by V. Todd), 4-7. UKIC, London

Thornton, J. 1991. The use of non-traditional materials in conservation. in *Gilded Wood: Conservation and History* (ed. D. Bigelow *et al*), 217-28. Madison, Connecticut

A CONSISTENT APPROACH TO A VARIED COLLECTION

Jonathan Ashley-Smith
Victoria and Albert Museum, South Kensington, London SW7 2RL

The Victoria and Albert Museum has large and varied collections, encompassing a wide range of materials and object types. The Conservation Department is also large and varied and has demonstrated a wide variation in attitudes to restoration. This paper describes the reasons for this variety and discusses the attempts that have been made to bring a consistent approach to the subject.

The words 'conservation' and 'restoration' are like all other words in that they may have many meanings and these meanings may change with time and vary with context. The two words are often juxtaposed as if they were opposites, mutually exclusive, like 'white' and 'black', with similar connotations of good and bad. However, the word 'conserve' has for a long time been used indiscriminately merely to mean treat without clear explanation of the nature or extent of that treatment. Conservation treatment will often involve an element of renewal, and it is possible to restore an object without compromising its conservation. Yet, despite this ambiguity, there is a common understanding of which practices might be described as tending toward restoration and which would be described as tending towards 'pure' conservation. To this extent the words are used to describe the extremes of a continuum of behaviour.

It might be expected that at one point in time all the practitioners within a single institution would be treating objects in the same fashion. That is, the observed behaviours within a single conservation department would be represented by a small and definable segment of this continuum. However, at the Victoria and Albert Museum a wide range of behaviour, spreading from one extreme to the other, has been observed.

The Conservation Department at the Victoria and Albert Museum was formally established in 1960 and the first Head of Department, Norman Brommelle, was entitled Keeper of Conservation. This tautological title indicated that preservation was as important as restoration. Yet the creation of a single department was to some extent part of a historic movement that perpetuated great differences in the way that different disciplines viewed the ethics of restoration.

Since the establishment of the Museum in 1852 there had been craftsmen whose job was restoration. They were originally called repairers. The few records of their work contain expressions such as 'mend', 'clean' and 'repair', but their decision-making processes were not recorded. During the first century of the Museum's existence the level of documentation about discussions of possible treatments is greatest for paintings and is quite thorough for important works of art such as the Raphael cartoons. Historically some types of object are deemed more important than others and treatment of these important objects is the subject of discussion. There is some correlation between discussion and sensible decision making about treatment. The ethics of conservation is about dialogue.

The conservation disciplines that have evolved in museums in Britain derive from distinctly different backgrounds of craft industry and domestic service (Daniels and Shashoua 1991). Each discipline brings with it certain 'baggage': the intellectual prestige of fine art, the servile nature of mending clothes, the commercial pressures of bookbinding. Where there is no point of communication between disciplines the baggage will remain, and may get heavier. After the Second World War there was a notable class gulf between the curator/owner and the craftsman/conservator. Only in the field of paintings and sculpture was there sufficient intellectual interest in the outcome of treatment to allow a dialogue that bridged this class barrier.

The collections at the Victoria and Albert Museum are large and extremely varied. By the mid 1970s the collections had been divided between twelve distinct departments each with its own specialist curatorial staff. Curatorial offices were created in isolated areas throughout the museum site. As the

Conservation Department expanded, craftsmen who had worked close by the curators were moved to a common work area. As numbers increased, craftsmen from different disciplines, who had formerly worked in the same room, moved to their own specialist studios. During the 1970s the number of specialist conservation sections rose from six to ten. This isolation of curator from curator, conservator from conservator, and conservator from curator, led to a situation where practices, already distinct, were likely to remain unchanged, or might even diverge further. They were very unlikely to converge spontaneously towards a consistent approach to treatment.

A contributory factor to this isolation has been the tendency to very long careers in national museums, thirty to forty years service in one department being common. Another factor has been the absence of specific training courses in conservation. This has meant that long-serving isolated craftsmen could pass on their ethical prejudices to innocent youngsters, who would in turn become long-serving isolated conservators.

The development of post-graduate training in conservation at the Victoria and albert Museum during the 1970s and 1980s catalysed the union of these isolated groups. Young people with independent and questioning minds, who were not necessarily inclined to become 'lifers', were joined by the unifying bond of studentship while they maintained loyalty to a specialist discipline. The employment of qualified middle-class youngsters in decorative arts disciplines gave objects conservators the status necessary to enter dialogue with the curators.

It was one of these students that gave the recently appointed Keeper of Conservation (Jonathan Ashley-Smith) the idea of writing a code of ethics that was specific to the Victoria and Albert Museum, but which would be relevant to all the different disciplines in the Department. A small working group[1], which included this student and scientists and conservators both old and young, eventually produced a four page document which the whole department was compelled to comment on. It was issued to all sections as part of a departmental handbook and has been used annually in the training of new students.

Being specific to the Victoria and Albert Museum it was possible to make the document slightly more explicit than the rather bland and general UKIC Guidance for Conservation Practice which was published at around the same time (1981). Thus while the UKIC guidance deals with Treatment in two sentences, the Victoria and Albert Museum Code of Practice has eleven separate points, three of them relating to the single subject of the limitations of the principles of reversibility. The UKIC document has only one sentence about restoration: 'It is unethical to modify or conceal the original nature of an object through restoration.' The Victoria and Albert Museum code has five paragraphs starting with the observation that 'Restoration may be an integral part of the conservation treatment', and ending with the pithy statement that 'Restoration need not be conspicuous, but the extent of restoration must be detectable without reference to documentation.'

However, even such specific guidance did not completely remove the differences between different studios; 'Paintings' replaced lost pigment on pictures but 'Sculpture' did not do so on polychromed wood. 'Furniture' replaced veneers invisibly but 'Textiles' did not reweave tapestries.

Twelve years later, in 1993, Dr Sue Wilsmore[2], a philosopher with an interest in the ethics of conservation, was invited to the Department. She interviewed staff and confirmed this disparity of attitude. She was integral to the organisation of a two-day workshop in which a large number of conservators and a handful of curators participated. The programme was designed to show the range of problems facing Victoria and Albert Museum conservators and the different approaches to decision making that could be used in interventive treatments (Lambert 1994; Richmond 1994).

The Workshop was a stimulating event which encouraged a new wave of thought about the criteria used to determine a suitable and ethical treatment. A working group[3] was established which was given the brief of constructing a check-list of criteria to be consulted before treatment. The first draft is reproduced at the end of this paper.

It is imperative that the enthusiasm generated by the Workshop and the subsequent discussions is maintained. Amongst the next stages is the proposal for a second workshop with much greater participation by curators. Within the next two years a newly refurbished wing of the Victoria and Albert Museum will be opened. Dubbed the 'Centre of Research and Conservation for the Decorative Arts' it will house most of the conservation studios and many of the curatorial offices. This will remove many of the old geographical barriers to dialogue. The recent organisational restructuring of the Conservation Department has as one of its aims the breaking down of barriers between conservation disciplines. It will be interesting to see whether in a further twelve years time the present spate of discussion and the proposed physical and organisational changes will have brought about a truly consistent approach to the treatment of a varied collection.

NOTES

1. Jonathan Ashley-Smith, Margaret Dobbie, Tim Miller, Anne Moncrieff, Jim Murrell, Nick Umney

2. S J W & Associates International, 27 Queen Court, Queen Square, Bloomsbury, London WC1N 3BB

3. Richard Cook, Helen Jones, Graham Martin, Alison Richmond, Nick Umney

REFERENCES

Daniels, V. and Shashoua, Y. 1991. Wet Cleaning of Paper and Textiles: Similarities and Differences. in *Paper and Textiles, The Common Ground*, (ed. L. Eaton), 19-27. SSCR, Glasgow

Lambert, S. 1994. A curator's view of the Ethics Workshop. *V & A Conservation Journal*, **10**, 8-9

Richmond, A. 1994. Conservation Ethics Workshop. *V & A Conservation Journal*, **10**, 4-7

VICTORIA AND ALBERT MUSEUM CONSERVATION DEPARTMENT

USING THE ETHICS CHECKLIST

This checklist of ethical considerations is intended to act as the 'conscience' of the conservation professional. It raises questions, but will not necessarily provide straightforward answers. Thinking about ethics is not a separate activity and throughout any conservation activity the list should prompt the basic question: 'Am I doing the right thing?' The conservation professional is expected to exercise the judgement gained through training and experience in deciding what is reasonable and acceptable to the profession.

The checklist is applicable to a broad range of conservation activities, not just interventive treatment of individual objects. The whole list should be used before, during and after any action/s; each question is equally valid.

A few definitions are necessary here to avoid confusion and repetition:

Action   - any process which the conservation professional may employ and which affects the objects under consideration. These include interventive treatment, preventive conservation measures, examination and study, sampling, analysis and **doing nothing**.

Clients - includes V&A Curators, other V&A Departments (including Conservation), the public, students, private owners.

Peers   - other conservation professional (conservators, conservation scientists, conservation managers and trainers), other museum and academic professionals (eg curators, art historians, scientists) both internal and external to the V&A.

A background document will be prepared for the Conservation Departmental Library. This will provide a commentary on the checklist and the reasoning behind its present form. It is expected that the list will be revised regularly.

ETHICS CHECKLIST

A   Why is action needed?

B   Have I consulted all existing records?

C   Do I need to consult any of the following: - clients - peers - other specialists?

D   Have I considered all the factors contributing to the identity and significance of the object/s: - historical - technical - associations - sacred - maker's intention?

E   What effect will my action/s have on the evidence of these factors?

F   Do I have sufficient information and skill to assess and implement action/s?

G   What are my options for action which will produce an acceptable result with minimum intervention?

H   What are the advantages and disadvantages of each course of action?

I   Can the use or environment be adapted instead of intervening on the object/s?

J   What are the resource implications of my action/s, and is my intended action the best use of resources?

K   Do established courses of action need to be adapted or new ones developed?

L   Are all my actions fully documented to a known and accepted standard: - images - written - on object/s?

M   Are my records accessible to appropriate users?

N   How will my action/s affect subsequent action/s?

O   Have I taken into account the future use and location of the objects/s?

P   How will I assess the success of the action/s, and how will I get feedback from clients and peers?

THE CARE OF RUGS AND CARPETS: THE CASE FOR CONSERVATION

Sharon E. Manitta
Carpet Conservation Workshop, Unit 2, Danebury Court,
Old Sarum Park, Salisbury, Wiltshire, SP4 6EB

WHAT ARE WE TALKING ABOUT?

Conserve - restore - repair - preserve ... what do these words really mean? The first two words will be defined before discussing the use of conservation for the care of rugs and carpets. It is important to clarify what is meant by conservation of textiles and even more importantly, what is *not* meant.

Outside the field of conservation, restoration and conservation are often seen as interchangeable terms. The profession, however, distinguishes between them, but, depending on the specialisation and who uses the term, there seem to be widely varying definitions from one practitioner to another. There are even more discrepancies among those outside conservation but inside what is loosely called the 'Heritage Business'. Trying to use these terms in another language can add more chaos to the vocabulary nightmare.

For the purposes of this paper, conservation will be defined using information derived from the codes of practice for conservation of various countries, from textile conservation studies and from experience and observations gained by working in this field - both in museums and now at a private conservation workshop. In addition, respected rug and carpet restorers have been consulted to learn about their views on conservation, how they define conservation and restoration, and what procedures they would use to repair a woven floor covering.

In its broadest terms, conservation of textiles is the ethical preservation of the true nature of an object. It includes hands-on work to stabilise, proper display (if needed), and environmental advice so that the object can be returned to use (whether that is in a passive or an active situation). The process of conservation attempts to slow down the deterioration of textiles while working within a set of criteria set down by fellow conservators.

The guidelines include:

- 'total respect for the physical, historic and aesthetic integrity of the object' and its future (UKIC 1990);
- treatments of a high standard that are ideally reversible;
- full documentation of the object and the treatment;
- ideally, not removing anything from the object or adding anything that in the future could possibly be mistaken as part of the original object;
- availability of information about treatments to other conservators;
- not relating quality of treatment to the monetary value of an object (AIC 1993).

Defining a textile conservator is difficult. Training in this field has developed in the last half of this century from informal apprenticeships at museums and workshops, to include both a more formalised apprenticeship system with supporting courses, and full-time postgraduate studies.

It is important to note that not all people who work in a conservation workshop, however skilled they may be in various aspects of the work, are conservators.

It would be safe to define a textile conservator as someone with scientific and historical knowledge of textiles, as well as textile techniques, and who can, through training and experience, assess the needs of an object, document them and carry out the hands-on work needed to preserve that object. A textile conservator must have the ability to carry out at least basic analysis of the condition of a range of objects, to clean those objects safely, to dye any necessary conservation materials and to carry out support work, as well as having the knowledge to advise on the objects' display, storage and environmental requirements and, not least, accept full responsibility for all of these.

Textile conservator is not an umbrella term to define anyone who stitches or sticks a textile together. On the other hand, a genuine conservator is not someone living in an 'airy-fairy' world. Whether the work is for a museum or for a more active existence, a conservator must deal with the realities of the object's use.

In a restorer's opinion, rugs and carpets need to be completely whole. This entails full infill of lost pile, foundation, side-cords and fringe. The piece is returned to the client looking as close to new as possible. It is difficult to tell what repairs have been done unless the object is seen before the restoration work was carried out.

Restoration attempts to put something back to what it is presumed to have looked like when new. To a conservator, restoration means more intervention to a piece, which could mean the loss of scientific, historical and technical information. And to a restorer, the use of the term conservation seems to centre around supporting an object on linen. To a restorer, if you do this, you are a conservator.

WHAT REALLY TAKES PLACE?

In some areas of textile treatment, the terms conservation and restoration seem worlds apart, but. in the case of rugs and carpets, some areas are closely associated. Can the 'airy-fairy' world of textile conservation (as it is sometimes perceived) deal with the realities of returning rugs and carpets to use in 'Historic Homes' as well as domestic use? Yes it can - and successfully.

Of course, no responsible conservator or restorer would put a fragile, vulnerable piece back into use on a floor, but many pieces which have incurred damage can be treated within the tenets of conservation. Examination, documentation, analysis, understanding of the client's wishes and future use of the object are important steps to treating a rug or carpet. A conservation workshop will also want to try to find out what has caused the damage and what restoration or other repair work has been done to a carpet in the past. While a rug restorer may check the colour-fastness of some or all colours in water, a conservator will also look at pH levels, types of dye, and the effects of various types and combinations of waters and detergency on the dyes and fibres.

Perhaps the best way to explain this process is to describe the actual treatment of a carpet at the Carpet Conservation Workshop.

A late eighteenth-century Axminster in private ownership was sent to the workshop for assessment, recommendation and treatment. The carpet measures 8.37m x 5.69m. It was woven with a wool and flax foundation and the wool pile is hand-knotted. The piece had large areas of damage. The brittleness of the flax had caused deterioration across the carpet which caused multiple splits. Where the pile was worn and the flax wefts broken, there were large areas of exposed warps which had started to split. The carpet was also soiled, stained and had areas of encrustation.

All this was exacerbated by previous attempts to keep this lovely carpet intact. Glued patches had been added and sometimes sewn through. The most damaging work had been the addition of strips of hessian across the entire back. These were glued and repaired with various adhesives and stuck in place in a haphazard manner which caused bagging and folds on the front.

The application of glue to carpets is a problem coming more and more to the attention of conservators. Glue leads to a number of problems when used on textiles and specifically carpets and rugs. It reduces flexibility, causing splitting and can cause distortion which may develop into the breakage of fibres. There can also be a reaction between the adhesive polymers and the dyes.

Natural glue is a good food source for some insects. Synthetic adhesives can remain tacky for a very long time, and while tacky they attract dust and pollutants. There is also the possibility of reaction with other substances in close proximity, such as floor polish or paint. The removal of the glue would be the most problematic part of the work so a careful work-plan had to be observed.

The front of the carpet was photographed and surface cleaned. In the conservation of textiles, surface cleaning means dry, low-powered vacuum suction, whereas restorers seem to use this term for a type of light wet-cleaning. The aim of this cleaning procedure was to remove as much loose dirt as possible - a positive benefit for the carpet as well as reducing the possibility of dirt masking the results of the testing. Next the carpet was turned and the hessian was carefully removed (this was quite easily done by manually peeling it off) to allow documentation of the back.

Documentation is an important tool in conservation and the size of this piece and its extensive and varied damage meant that the information had to be thoroughly recorded. The back was mapped - a daunting task, as some areas had different layers of more than one type of glue, various materials used for patches (bits of cotton, carpet tape, paper) and numerous types of splits, areas of loss, holes, etc. The extensive use of documentation is another difference between conservation and restoration.

Once the mapping and other documentation was completed, testing began so that the best method of glue removal could be formulated. 'Best' meant a treatment that was effective, yet safe for the carpet and for the people doing the work. The glues had to be identified, by testing to see if they were natural or synthetic, before the method of removal was decided upon.

Only one type of glue was water soluble; others reacted to solvents by swelling and then re-hardening. Unfortunately, in their swollen state, they still were not easy to remove and tended to seep further into the carpet fibres. One glue was identified as latex and there was discussion about using the latex removal treatment developed at the Smithsonian Institution in Washington (Ballard 1987). However, this requires the use of 1,1,1-trichloroethane which is now being phased out on health and safety grounds, and, even if allowed would be difficult to use for such a large piece.

A more 'minimalist' treatment for the glue removal was used. It was possible to remove the small patches except for areas which had been stitched. This was done by covering the patch with an absorbent paper and applying gentle heat. There was a possibility of the adhesive sinking deeper into the carpet once it was more viscous, but the results were quite successful and a great deal of adhesive was removed. The patches were then peeled away. Two procedures were then used on the remaining glue covering most of the back of the carpet. This fell into three tactile categories: a dry white adhesive that felt crystalline to the touch, a hard yellow glue found mainly on the back of the cotton patches and the latex glue. The yellow glue was water soluble and was easily removed.

During testing, it had been observed that the white glue could easily be removed with gentle abrasion. While abrasion is usually something conservators try to avoid, in this case careful abrasion with plastic spatulas effectively removed most of the white glue. While this procedure may seem an unskilled job, the workroom assistants carrying it out had to assess constantly the effect on the weave of the carpet and the state of the damaged materials.

The removal of the latex was done with a very low-tech procedure, but it was not used until assessed by a number of conservation criteria. It was decided to remove the latex by laying an absorbent paper (as neutral as possible) over an area and using a 'cool' iron on top of the paper to slightly melt the adhesive, so that it was absorbed by the paper.

Although this meant applying some heat to brittle fibres and running the risk that softening the glue might mean that some could be absorbed further into the foundation, it was felt that this was the best procedure under the circumstances or, as often in conservation, the least damaging. The glue came off more easily than expected and very little seemed to have spread or seeped into the foundation. When the blotting procedure was completed and the remaining glue had dried, the formerly tacky areas underwent the same procedure.

If the glues had been left, the necessary support stitching would have had to be carried out through hard and sticky areas. This would have caused more stress to the piece and the lack of flexibility would have made the treatment, in many areas, redundant.

The carpet was surface cleaned once more and then wet-cleaned using a flood-wash treatment (Plate 1). When dry, the carpet was fully supported on to linen holland and re-warped where necessary. The warps were couched down. To protect the exposed warps and other weak areas, brick stitching was worked, using wool dyed sympathetically to match the pile. No re-piling took place. While the carpet now looks whole and complete, upon very close inspection, whether by sight or by touch, the completed conservation can be identified (Plate 2).

The piece will be returned to moderate domestic use.

WHY ALL THE FUSS?

Does it matter whether repairs can be identified? Are we being too precious?

Certainly, there is a fine balance between the 'don't-breathe-on-things' school of conservation and the realities of knowing that things have to be viewed in museums by numbers of people and, even in private ownership, objects have to hold a decorative or display value in exposed environments, even if not actually used.

The ethos of good conservation is to keep an object 'alive' for the future by doing appropriate work and doing it in a way that will, hopefully, be understood by future generations. Conservators must not cheat history by trying to interpret the past through our late twentieth-century eyes. Most textile conservators do want to avoid the less acceptable restoration practices of the past. But these practices (which may have been influenced by the commercial pressures put on restorers as well as by their more craft-based treatments) may become tempting for some conservators now that they are doing more private work. That is, conservators are facing the same financial constraints in their work for museums as they are for private clients.

In March 1993, the Textile Section of UKIC discussed some of these problems. How can exchange of information continue when conservators are competing against each other and against those who, by unethical practices, would undercut them in competitive tendering? Can corners be cut and a 'proper job' still be done? Dealers and auction houses often complain that documentation is a waste of time. Money is always a factor; clients want jobs done as cheaply as possible, especially when they do not understand the problems of the care of textiles. Of course, one can go overboard, but good documentation is the key to knowing what work is needed and to conveying this clearly to your client, as well as amassing important information for collectors, museums and other conservators.

The customer must appreciate other aspects of conservation. For example, testing is an expensive and sometimes time-consuming procedure, reliant on skilled staff and costly equipment.

But before trying to inform the public about what conservators do, it is important to agree what is meant by conservation, so that the present confusion is reduced. More than once, after a public lecture, someone has said, 'I had no idea what went into textile conservation. I thought you just had to know how to sew'!

An accreditation system is needed. At present, there are people purporting to be conservators who would not be recognised by genuine conservators. Until there is a recognisable qualification, there will continue to be a real possibility that the conservation world will be open to abuse.

Once the profession can clearly state to people what conservation offers, the customer can decide whether they wish to have their rugs and carpets restored or conserved. It is to be hoped that once they understand what conservation has to offer, they will choose conservation.

BIBLIOGRAPHY

AIC (American Institute of Conservation) 1993. *Code of Ethics*. Washington

Ballard, M. 1987. The Removal of cross-linked synthetic latex from carpets. in Preprints from ICOM Committee for Conservation: 8th Triennial Meeting, Sydney, Australia, 6-11 September 1987, Vol 1, 331-8. The Getty Conservation Institute, Los Angeles

UKIC, 1990. *Guidance for Conservation Practice*. London

Plate 1   Wet cleaning of the Chatsworth carpet

Plate 2   Chatsworth carpet after cleaning

RESTORATION AND CONSERVATION - ISSUES FOR CONSERVATORS: A TEXTILE CONSERVATION PERSPECTIVE

Mary Brooks, Caroline Clark, Dinah Eastop and Carla Petschek
The Textile Conservation Centre, Apartment 22, Hampton Court Palace,
East Molesey, Surrey KT8 9AU

INTRODUCTION

The view that conservation belongs in museums and restoration outside them is not uncommon. Very often, depending on the speaker and the context, either or both of these emotive and judgmental terms is used in a pejorative sense. Reality, however, is more complex.

Clear definitions are essential for an understanding and discussion of the relative merits and demerits of these two concepts. Such definitions are not easy and are made more complex by slipshod daily use. Restoration and conservation are sometimes presented as totally opposed ideals. Elsewhere, they are used as synonymous terms. Beck's recent book, which criticises various painting treatments, provides a good example of this confused usage: 'Restoration, *per se*, is sometimes not merely desirable, but actually essential; nothing said in the following pages should be understood as a rejection of necessary conservation.' (Beck and Daley 1993)

Here Beck implies that acceptable 'restoration' is actually 'necessary conservation'. Further confusion can be added by the association of restoration with 'old-fashioned' techniques and conservation with 'modern' technology. Yet more ambiguities arise, particularly in Europe, for language reasons. The French word *restaurateur* is equivalent to the word 'conservator' in English, whereas the French word *conservateur* is equivalent to the English term 'curator' or 'keeper'. French conservators are hoping to adopt the term *conservateur-restaurateur*.

Various guidelines have sought to clarify and identify the meaning of 'conservation' but there are interesting divergences between them. The distinctions between the various codes developed by different national conservation organisations have been discussed by Dinah Eastop (1993). It is clear that there is no current international agreement on the key elements defining the activity of conservation. It is also clear that some fundamental rethinking is going on. This is particularly true where the ideal of reversibility, once seen as an essential distinction between conservation and restoration, is concerned. The *Code of Ethics and Guidance for Conservation Practice* of the Australian Institute for the Conservation of Cultural Material does not cite reversibility as a conservation criterion (AICCM 1986). The American Institute of Conservation dropped reversibility as a criterion in their recent revision of the *Code of Ethics and Standards of Practice* (AIC 1993) although it had been included in the 1979 version (AIC 1979). Practical problems, such as the compatibility of the ideals of reversibility with treatments such as wet cleaning, have led to re-evaluation. The ideal of minimal removal of original material and minimal additions seems to be replacing reversibility as a standard of conduct and practice. Michael Corfield, in discussing developing standards in the UK quotes one phrase from the United Kingdom Institute for Conservation's 1983 *Guidance for Conservation Practice* as unifying all forms of conservation in a single sentence: 'Conservation is the means by which the true nature of an object is preserved.' (Corfield 1988).

Both textile conservation and textile restoration involve intervention - a physical modification of the textile with the intention of preserving or enhancing it physically and/or visually. In neither case can the original state of the textile be recreated. Conservation aims to maintain the integrity of the object physically and visually while removing and adding the minimum material. Restoration has different orders of priority. The visual or functional is paramount. Restoration aims to recreate the visual and physical appearance of the textile as it is originally believed to have looked. This also raises the interesting question of the distinction between a restored textile and a fake. Does this depend on the actual treatment carried out, or on the way in which the treated piece is presented to the public? The issue of fakes was explored extensively in the exhibition *Fakes? The Art of Deception* at the British Museum and will not be discussed further in this paper (Jones 1990).

It is essential to accept that both treatments change a textile in some way. This paper argues that conservation and restoration are very different concepts which are expressed through different approaches but which can work together for the ultimate benefit of the textile.

CULTURAL ATTITUDES TO CONSERVATION AND RESTORATION

Attitudes to conservation and restoration are the products of a particular culture. Approaches vary both within and across cultures.

Ceremonial textiles highlight this issue. Different cultural requirements are made by the heritage community, in the person of the conservator or restorer, and by the community which created, revere and may still use the artefacts. Approaches to the complex problems of the correct protocol for dealing with such artefacts have recently become more defined. As an example, mutually acceptable approaches to *Taonga* (Maori treasures) in *Aotearoa* (New Zealand) have been discussed by Tracey Wedge (1993). The 1985 *Code of Ethics* of the New Zealand Professional Conservators' Group balances care for the object with the need for access by users, explicitly acknowledging the continuing sacred function of the textiles (NZPCG 1991).

The Oriental approach to preservation of its cultural heritage differs from that of the West. Some of the complex cultural issues behind these vastly different approaches have been discussed by Mary Greenacre. Although there is a common ideal in the commitment to 'relic restoring without creation', a different appreciation of the object can result in equally valid but varied treatment approaches (Greenacre 1988). Treatments of the silk borders of painted *thang-kas* may serve as an example. A Western approach would, typically, retain the original degraded silk and support it on specially dyed new fabric. In contrast, in Japan, the original silk is sometimes removed and replaced with deliberately light-aged modern silk (Hofenk de Graef 1993).

Many countries have a long tradition of restoration, sometimes carried out by the makers of the textile. In France, the state-run Manufacture des Gobelins has always restored its own tapestries in its own workshops in a closed tradition. Wendy Hefford has examined expenditure on cleaning, restoration and relining of English State tapestries. The Vanderbank family tapestry workshop cleaned, repaired and enlarged their own tapestries over several generations. In 1707-8, the workshop enlarged the Vanderbank Dutch Boors tapestry at Kensington Palace by 'knotting ye warp threads together of all said pces with the materials like old work' (Hefford 1976). There are other long traditions of restoration as everyday maintenance. For example, ecclesiastical textiles have traditionally been repaired and renewed by nuns for religious use. This may have been appropriate for ecclesiastical textiles but was less suitable for military colours which were also often sent to nunneries or private embroidery workshops for repairs. Sometimes restoration has been a political imperative. The former USSR funded total restoration of destroyed palaces. The interiors of the Kuskovo Palace have been rehung with copies of the original damasks, woven using the same threads and dyes, at the Novospassky Monastery textile department (Hughes 1987).

CHANGING ATTITUDES TO TEXTILE CONSERVATION AND RESTORATION

It is also important to recognise the influence of fashion. How much has the development of a different aesthetic of the past, exemplified by the approach of the National Trust at Calke Abbey, Derbyshire, and English Heritage at Brodsworth, Yorkshire, subtly altered attitudes to previous repairs? With this shift in opinion, evidence of alterations, use and abuse is more likely to be tolerated or even welcomed. In a fine arts context, the requirement for a conservation or restoration treatment is more likely to be for a preservation technique which ensures that the textile appears complete and well defined in terms of imagery and structure. A social history institution is more likely to accept evidence of alterations and want them retained or even self-evident. These shifts will make a fascinating study for future cultural historians but they are already influencing our current practices. A recent article examines the implications of connoisseurship attitudes for conservators (Orlofsky and Trupin 1993).

The financial value attached to a textile may also make a difference to conservation and restoration choices. A well-known rug and carpet dealer is quite clear about the financial implications of good restoration: 'A good repair using the best quality wool available and the best colour is essential for the dealer to sell with confidence (and) for the restorer to charge adequately.' (Anon 1993)

Rather than forcing quality down, as many fear that competitive tendering will do, financial pressure here would appear to be forcing up the quality of work. The implications of competitive tendering in this context are discussed below.

Historically, textile conservation developed out of restoration traditions and techniques. Both approaches depend on a common foundation, using hands-on skills to implement the chosen intervention. Disturbed at the loss of information implicit in restoration approaches and convinced of the need to interfere as little as possible, conservation concepts slowly developed to give an alternative approach to treating historic textiles. These growing conservation ideas reflected changing ideas about the key elements in a textile and the role required of historic textiles. This was coupled with an increasing awareness of problems with materials used in both restoration and conservation. Old repairs vividly demonstrated problems with shifting non-fast dyes. Physical stress and damage resulted from some conservation work using early adhesives with consequent reviews of the concept of reversibility and treatment modifications. Such problems were noted by Karen Finch in her account of the degradation over twenty years of an adhesive applied to a tapestry in 1960 (Finch 1980).

The critical distinction between the two inter-linked approaches lies in the objective of the intervention. Conservation focuses on the overall integrity of the textile. In restoration treatments, the need to recreate the visual effect or function is dominant. The question now is whether these two traditions will continue to diverge or if synergy can be developed to evolve a more flexible and effective palate of textile treatments combining elements of both approaches. In order to evaluate either or both of these approaches, it is necessary to step back and ask why our culture wishes to preserve textiles at all.

WHAT ARE WE TRYING TO PRESERVE?

This is a fundamental issue. It involves an evaluation of why our culture wishes to preserve textiles and what elements are considered to be important. The value placed on these elements justifies the expenditure of time, energy and money in restoration or conservation.

Some textiles, such as the hat/mask worn by Mr Merrick ('The Elephant Man') are preserved because of their historic, social, or political context rather than because of their intrinsic beauty or financial value (TCC Ref.1845.2). For other textiles, aesthetic value or inherent technological interest are justifications for preservation. A 1950s nightdress in Ardil, a little known regenerated protein fibre made from peanuts, is a good example of technological interest justifying the preservation of an otherwise unremarkable garment (Brooks 1993a). The financial value placed on textiles such as tapestries, carpets and *opus anglicanum*, historically sometimes considered more valuable than paintings, has helped to ensure their survival.

The motive behind the impulse for preservation depends on an explicit or implicit evaluation of the meaning of the textile. This may reside in different elements. The relative value placed on these elements often influences decisions made in the restoration or conservation process. For some textiles, such as curtains, the function is of major importance. In others, imagery is considered more significant than the construction or the fabric support. Appliqué vestments, palls, and Torah mantles are typical examples. The fibre, weave, pigment or dye could be the most important element in an ethnographic or archaeological textile. Over and above these factors, the nature of the textile influences the type and degree of conservation or restoration which is possible.

The visual image, whether in terms of design and pattern or of cut and construction, cannot always be separated from the medium. In a woven structure, such as a tapestry, the construction and the design are one and the same. The approach to treating past repairs and holes in such a structure may have radical implications for the interpretation of the imagery as well as for the physical stability of the piece. Similarly, the difference between a painted textile and a painting on a textile support has recently been much debated (AIC 1991). Flexibility, drape and handle have been identified as critical requirements in the treatment of a painted banner but may be irrelevant in the treatment of a stretched and framed painted canvas.

Archaeological textiles are important not just for their intrinsic interest but for evidence they may supply about fibre availability and trading, dye technology, weaving expertise and social practices of a particular culture. Staining may be evidence of particular burial techniques and any approach which seeks to remove such evidence is unacceptable. Jennifer Barnett describes the treatment of one of nine 'shirts', dated to the Fifth Dynasty (2494-2345 BC) and excavated at Deshasheh by Petrie in 1898. She lists the questions she asked when assessing the value of soiling as evidence of Old Kingdom mummification and burial techniques when compared to their possible degradative effects. The presence of natron, bitumen, a gelatinous glue, resins and waxes was deduced. She concluded that cleaning was inappropriate: 'In view of ... the rarity of both the garment and the substances on it, it seems that, in this case, washing is inappropriate because it would remove significant historical evidence. This takes precedence over the importance of restoring the original appearance of the garment (including possible natural pleating) by washing.' (Barnett 1983)

Costume offers a complex range of information about past social behaviour and aesthetics as well as technological and construction methods. It also requires presentation in a way which allows the three-dimensional form to be read appropriately. The implications of this need are discussed later in this paper. The objectives of treatment need to be clearly defined, particularly where past alterations and repairs are concerned.

Doré's paper on the conservation of two eighteenth-century court dresses in the collection of the Victoria and Albert Museum is both unusual and useful in stating explicitly the museum's policy at that time on previous alterations and the replacement of missing parts: 'In the Victoria and Albert Museum the rule is that, if at all possible, the garment will be returned to its earliest condition, providing there is sufficient left to make a reasonably complete whole, and the alterations are not in themselves of historic importance.' She concludes that '... replacements of missing pieces (one could almost say restoration) are an aid to public appreciation of costume, providing they are as historically accurate as possible, but not so perfect that they could mislead an expert ... .' (Doré 1978)

CONSERVATION AND RESTORATION: PROBLEMS AND BENEFITS

It is necessary to accept that there is an element of the subjective in both conservation and restoration treatments. Both are, explicitly or implicitly, interpreting the textile but with different intentions. This highlights the importance of the ideal of a shared approach for both conservators and restorers. Initial preliminary research, including dialogue with the relevant curator/client/owner, is critical together with complete documentation of all treatment objectives, interventions and materials. Future generations of textile scholars and museum visitors should not be compromised in their understanding and appreciation of a textile as a result of treatment by our generation.

Problems experienced with restoration and conservation

Both restoration and conservation depend on the understanding and practical skill of the practitioner and the use of suitable materials. Poor quality work results in poor treatments, to the ultimate detriment of the textile. Improperly understood or misapplied materials and poor fibre and colour matches result in more physical and visual disfigurement rather than less. Historically, restorers are less likely to carry out detailed analysis of a textile or provide documentation of their treatments.

The main issue specifically relating to restoration is that of the loss of the integrity of an object. This results in a consequent loss of information and associated difficulties of interpretation and misinterpretation. The tradition of tapestry reweaving demonstrates the practical and ethical issues involved here. Paradoxically, in order to start an effective rewoven restoration, it is necessary to remove weak areas so that the new work can begin on firm foundations. Clearly this removal of original material, although weak, would be unacceptable from a conservation point of view. Some restoration techniques may enable a complete and effective recreation of what is believed to be the original image and colour, but at the expense of the original technique. The Werkplaats tot Herstel van Antiek Textiel in Holland has been restoring the State Tapestries of the Province of Zeeland for nearly 30 years. In order to ensure visual continuity, the final tapestries in the series are being treated in the same way as those started in the 1960s, but the technique will not be used again. The restoration was based on a careful copy of the existing design made prior to the removal of all silk areas. These sections were then recreated using a needleweaving technique. The resulting restoration gives a fine colourful image but it is clearly no longer the original tapestry (Brooks 1993b).

There are also design problems with infilling an area of loss. The restored design and colours may be based on assumptions or hazy reconstruction, thus changing the original image. Other restoration may deliberately change or 'improve' the original design which may itself give an insight into the morals or religious attitudes of one period to the art of a previous age. A fine seventeenth-century Brussels tapestry depicting *Anthony and Cleopatra* has been treated in this way, probably on the instructions of a nineteenth-century owner. Cleopatra was woven to show her draping a naked leg over Anthony's knee. The offending limb was later cut out and the resulting gap skilfully rewoven to match the red of Anthony's cloak. Unfortunately, the red dye has since faded to orange so the modest intention of the reweaving is now vividly confounded (TCC Ref. 0092; Collection of The Worshipful Company of Goldsmiths) (Plate 1).

Conservation faces similar problems in terms of interpretation of design in missing areas. Although conservators tend not to introduce design back into missing areas and use instead neutral or coloured support materials, these still impose a particular interpretation upon a textile. Conservation can be less effective in preserving the overall image. In some cases, the need to retain one important element, for example the image, may only be achieved at the expense of other textile properties, such as flexibility or drape. This can be a critical issue when treating textiles such as large painted banners. Conservation is less effective than restoration when dealing with certain textile structures such as knitting, crochet, net or lace. The treatment of a knitted shawl is discussed below.

Both restoration and conservation have high cost and time requirements. In certain cases, one option or the other may offer a quicker or cheaper route. Ideally the choice of treatment should not depend on financial constraints but on the long term needs of the textile in its particular context.

Benefits of restoration and conservation

Effective restoration can give a textile visual completeness and physical strength. It can be particularly successful for functional textiles, such as carpets and rugs, or three-dimensional pieces, such as upholstery or costume, where structure and line are critical. However, as discussed above, this may be at the expense of original materials or techniques. In contrast, conservation aims to retain the integrity of the textile as far as possible with the minimal removal of materials and minimal additions. The objective is to ensure that all materials used should be as stable as possible and that the treatment should 'fail' before the object does in order to reduce the risk of damaging the original through physical stress.

Retaining the historical evidence of use and abuse is important in a conservation treatment. For example, 'doors' cut in tapestries are retained as important evidence of the use of a tapestry in a particular context. With some textiles, making the decision of 'how far to go' in retaining or removing the accretions of the past is complex and depends on effective dialogue with the custodian of the textile.

The conservation profession, although relatively new, has an increasingly formalised training structure. It is based on the premise of trained practitioners sharing a common base of knowledge and commitment to certain standards and guidelines. Publication of analysis, treatment, and documentation is regularly undertaken with the aim of improving treatment methods.

Conservators' responsibility often extends to the provision of a suitable future environment for the object. This may range from implementation of storage and display standards to providing display forms. At one extreme, work on acceptable handling, display and storage may be regarded as the purest form of conservation. The object itself is not compromised by an intervention but its future stability is ensured by a high standard of environmental protection. 'Doing nothing' may be the most effective strategy. However, this form of conservation may be the most difficult to implement. It is a critical aspect of conservation, extending far beyond restoration into the future standards of care, and is often the most cost and time effective strategy for the care of our collections.

THE DECISION-MAKING PROCESS IN CHOOSING AND DEVELOPING AN APPROPRIATE TEXTILE TREATMENT STRATEGY

The first stage for all those involved in the care of an object is to realise that there is a decision to be made. Overt debate on the various options between intervention and non-intervention, conservation and restoration, and the future care of the textile is vital. Once the intellectual decision identifying the critical elements of the textile has been taken, ideally as a result of consultation and collaboration between the curator and/or client and the conservator or restorer, other factors and constraints need to be considered.

These may include the following.

1. Clarification of the future role and function of the textile in its context

The 'use' to be made of a treated textile influences the degree of conservation and/or restoration to be implemented. The context (ownership and location of a textile in a museum, private collection or domestic setting) has obvious implications for the type of treatment desired. For example, a textile may be treated with different levels of intervention if it is going to function as a study piece with frequent handling, be placed in storage with minimum handling, or be displayed. Storage facilities and methods themselves, such as rolling, may affect the selection of an appropriate treatment technique.

2. Time pressure

Clearly, the speed with which a textile needs to be prepared for an exhibition or loan influences the quantity of treatment possible; it should not influence the quality.

3. Financial pressure/administrative requirements

Certain constraints such as competitive tendering, grant structures, or the need to spend up within the current financial year may influence the quantity of treatment possible, whether it is restoration or conservation. However, current competitive tendering processes also appear to place less stress on quality. The case for accepting the second lowest tender as a mechanism for ensuring high quality treatment has been suggested (Constantinides 1993). It is clear that the ability to carry out effective treatment, whether conservation or restoration, is dependent on a system which is conducive to quality work. There are situations, such as insurance requirements, which may tip the balance between a decision for restoration or conservation, or influence the degree of treatment which is permissible within terms of the funding.

The final decision whether to select a restoration or conservation treatment and the quantity of treatment possible should be a combination of these factors - balancing responsibility towards the textile and its continued role with realistic practical concerns.

AREAS OF LOSS

In the context of this debate it is particularly useful to consider alternative treatments for areas of loss. These present aesthetic and practical problems as they affect the visual, physical and functional aspects of a textile. An area of loss can so dominate a design that it destroys or distorts the intended visual effect. However, the notion of 'incompleteness' may be a culturally defined concept. Some cultures appear more willing to accept either a continual re-creation of the piece or missing areas. Experience indicates that there is a theoretical continuum between 'pure' conservation lying at one end and 'pure' restoration at the other. It is significant that the recent leaflet *Conservation - Restoration: The Options* (issued jointly by The Conservation Unit and Historic Scotland) emphasises, in bold type, that 'conservation and restoration are aspects of the same process.' (CU and Historic Scotland 1993)

Preventive conservation treatment, ensuring acceptable standards of handling, display, and storage, may be regarded as the 'purest' form of conservation. No intervention is carried out on the object itself but its future stability is ensured. In some cases, conservation is limited to ensuring structural stability alone. Restoration of the image is considered to be inappropriate. There may be insufficient information to recreate the design satisfactorily, or it is not thought to be a key element, or such intervention may be damaging. A textile's integrity could be compromised by forcing an unfounded interpretation.

As opposed to 'pure' conservation, 'pure' restoration is an interventive treatment which involves a complete recreation of the visual image or structure. As pointed out above, restoration techniques are used on certain textile structures where conservation would not be a workable aesthetic or physical option. The treatment chosen for an early machine-knitted silk shawl is a good example of restoration selected to meet the requirements of the client and the needs of the textile (TCC Ref. 1865). The desire of the private client to wear the shawl occasionally resulted in the decision to re-introduce structure into the holed areas. Cobbled repairs were removed as they were deemed visually and physically inappropriate. In these and other damaged areas, the construction technique was reformed manually with a needle using the original unravelled thread where possible or a visually sympathetic cotton thread (Plates 2-4).

Many preservation treatments lie somewhere in the middle area of the continuum. In some cases, it is appropriate to use restoration as part of the conservation treatment. This is a synergistic use of two techniques - a modified restoration technique is integrated within a conservation based intervention. The intention is to inform, not to deceive. This approach may be described as 'ethical restoration' and is particularly appropriate where the visual imagery of the textile is a key element. The following examples illustrate treatments which used combination techniques.

Two-dimensional textiles

The image, generally, is the most important element in a tapestry. It may be possible to appreciate an incomplete design but, in general, significant areas of loss can cause disinterest and confusion. A common problem with sixteenth-century tapestries is the loss of the dark outlines around the main figures which form a significant design element. This is due to the rapid degradation of wool dyed brown or black with an iron mordant. This inherent weakness can be further complicated by unskilled or unknowledgeable intervention.

In the case of the Brussels tapestry *The Triumph of Fortitude* many of the dark outlines had been cut out and the cut edges then sewn together. This resulted in a misrepresentation of the design as well as distortion of the weave structure. To resolve these problems, the cut areas were released from the repair stitches to ease the distortion. New wool warps were inserted to strengthen the structure. As the dark outlines are so integral to the visual image they were rewoven, so restoring the necessary bold visual line and structural strength (TCC Ref. 0424; The Board of Trustees of the National Museums and Galleries on Merseyside (Walker Art Gallery)) (Plate 5). This is an example of a restoration technique used within a conservation context.

The inappropriate filling of areas of loss caused by cuts, degradation or fungal attack often results in further disfigurement. Patches from other tapestries are sometimes added. The colour and texture may blend but the design is often a mismatch. One English tapestry with a popular seventeenth-century design of *Children at Play* illustrates this problem. It had suffered a large area of loss throughout the central group and background foliage. This had been patched using a fragment from another tapestry which did not correspond with the design. The decision to remove the patch and recreate the design was possible due to the existence of other tapestries woven to the same cartoon, but reweaving was not considered an acceptable option because of the need to remove original material in order to work from a firm foundation. The treatment chosen was to support the area with a stitched linen fabric backing. Stitching and colour choice took account of the structural needs of the tapestry and the design. The conservation stitches thus not only gave support but also helped to re-introduce the image. The conservation intervention blends into the overall structure and appearance of the tapestry, but is discernible to the knowledgeable eye (TCC Ref. 0769.b; Cotehele House, Cornwall,

The National Trust) (Plates 6,7). This is an example where a conservation technique was used because of the potentially damaging effect of restoration.

The need to ensure that the imagery of a textile is visually complete is illustrated by the 'ethical restoration' approach used when treating a set of 1925 Iron and Steel Trades Confederation silk banners painted with a water-based paint (TCC Ref. 1246.i-vi) (Conservation Services TCC 1993). One banner had particularly extensive losses in both the image and lettering. These missing letters were recreated by stitching in a new silk patch painted using printing inks. This patch can be removed thus reversing the treatment (Plates 8,9). The objective of the infilling was to re-establish the original pictorial significance of the banner.[1]

Three-dimensional textiles

The issues of preservation and restoration of three-dimensional textiles are highlighted in the case of nine fragments of twill-weave wool and eight buttons discovered in the backfill of a Leicestershire coal mine (TCC Ref. 1603; Leicestershire Museums, Arts and Records Service) (Gibson 1993). These proved to be part of a working man's waistcoat, initially dated to about 1700 but possibly as early as the fifteenth century. It was decided to display the fragments so as to provide a 'human interest' element alongside a collection of industrial machinery at Snibston Discovery Centre, Leicestershire. The identification of this display role had a major influence on the treatment strategy. The fragments and the evidence they contained needed to be safely preserved whilst being presented so that this 'human interest' element was explicit. Controlled reconstruction of the fragments was a main aim. Treatment included wet cleaning and a stitched support of the four main garment fragments to stabilise them and infill missing areas. This was a minimal treatment which aimed to retain the creases in the garment as evidence of wear and 'burial'.

Once the individual fragments had been stabilised, the 'restoration' or 'reconstruction' process began. This was a totally distinct process. It aimed to provide adequate structural support for the fragments while showing them as they were thought to be located when worn. A padded form of a stylised human torso was constructed to meet these apparently conflicting needs. The resulting display is a successful compromise. It enables the fragments to serve the role identified for them. The conservation report clearly states that the reconstruction is speculative and the technique employed allows the fragments to be removed without interfering with the conservation undertaken (Lister 1994) (Plates 10,11).

The need to evaluate restoration options is demonstrated by the treatment of an eighteenth-century dress (open gown and petticoat) belonging to Leicestershire County Museums, Art Galleries and Library Services. Examination of the materials, cut and construction of the dress showed that it had been altered extensively, most recently for fancy dress (Rollins 1992). The woven silk fabric, with a pattern of stripes and flowers, was dated to c.1765-75 and it was assumed that originally the dress had been cut in the style of c.1770. Subsequent alterations had led to the removal of significant areas of silk fabric, particularly at the top of the skirt. The dress was accepted into the museum's collection and given priority for conservation treatment because of its mid-eighteenth century date. It complemented the museum's costume collection by filling a chronological 'gap' and it was decided that the dress should be 'returned' to its earliest condition, (as was decided in the mid 1970s for two mantuas in the Victoria and Albert Museum) (Doré 1978).

Following detailed examination, analysis, and documentation of the dress in its existing condition, repairs and alterations were removed and the problem of replacing missing areas of silk fabric was addressed. After careful consideration, including the preparation of a full scale toile of the proposed 'restored' cut, the decision was made jointly by the conservator and curator to replace the missing areas with 'replica' fabric, printed in stripes to blend with the pattern-woven original. The addition of this custom-made fabric enabled the conservator to 'reverse' later alterations and thereby 'reconstruct' an eighteenth-century cut to the dress. These twentieth century modifications, unlike the earlier alterations, are well documented. The replica fabric blends well with the original when the dress is viewed as a whole. However, on close inspection it is obvious through the deliberate differences in technique and design - printing versus weaving and plain stripes versus floral stripes. The treatment of this dress, encompassing both conservation and restoration, enabled it to meet the role assigned to it, which is to present the style, as well as the fabrics and construction, of a fashionable dress of *c*.1770 (Plates 12-14).

Upholstery treatments present a complex range of decisions involving both restoration and conservation. Upholstered seat units are made up of layers of different fabric and fillings on a wooden frame. Failure in one element means that the whole unit suffers with consequent deformation of the seat profile. When the profile is considered as important as the overall stability, more interventive treatment may be necessary. This often involves removal of all layers for treatment and modification of the original method of application of the upholstery. Conservation treatments may be appropriate for individual layers but re-application and recreation of the original profile may require new materials to be integrated within the original structure.

In the case of an eighteenth-century settee, the insect-damaged wooden seat sub-frame, webbing, and upholstery were all weak and degraded. The curator and conservator together made the decision to remove the damaged sub-frame to safe storage as it was beyond treatment (TCC. Ref. 1643; English Heritage). All the upholstery layers were removed for conservation. A replica sub-frame was made. The conserved webbing was repositioned in the replica frame and new webbing was placed over the top to provide a discreet stable foundation for the conserved overlaying layers. New materials were integrated for added stability. The original application method was modified to reduce tension and stress upon the upholstery and frame. This combined technique of restoration and conservation enabled the recovery of the original profile of the seat.

CONCLUSION

Creative compromise is essential in evolving treatments which respect the needs of objects and their designated role. Effective decision-making and treatment depends on active and informed discussion between the conservator or restorer and the client or curator. The appropriate use of restoration practice has a part to play within the framework of conservation treatments and documentation so that artefacts can be preserved, understood and enjoyed.

NOTE

1.   The conservation of all six banners was assisted financially by the ISTC with the aim that each banner should be on permanent loan to a museum located within the district.

REFERENCES

AIC, 1979. *Code of Ethics and Standards for Practice.* The American Institute for Conservation of Historic and Artistic Works, Washington

AIC, 1991. *Postprints of the Joint Session of the Paintings and Textiles Speciality Groups.* The American Institute for Conservation, Washington

AIC, 1993. *Code of Ethics and Standards for Practice.* The American Institute for Conservation of Historic and Artistic Works, Washington

AICCM, 1986. *Code of Ethics and Guidance for Conservation Practice for those involved in the conservation of cultural material in Australia.* Australian Institute for the Conservation of Cultural Material, Canberra

Anon., 1993. Report on David Black's talk at Rug Restorers Association, 5 September 1993. *RRA Newsletter*, (No 8, October, 1993), no pagination

Barnett, J. 1983. *The Conservation of an Early Egyptian Funerary Garment.* Unpublished Diploma Report, Textile Conservation Centre/Courtauld Institute of Art

Beck, J. and Daley, M. 1993. *Art Restoration: The Culture, the Business and the Scandal,* ix-x. London

Brooks, M.M. 1993a. Ardil: The Disappearing Fibre? in *Saving the 20th Century. The Conservation of Modern Materials*, 81-91. CCI, Ottawa

Brooks, M.M. 1993b. *UKIC Textile Section visit to Textile Conservation Workshops in Holland.* unpublished report. Textile Conservation Centre

Conservation Services, General Department, TCC, 1993. Problems in the Conservation of a Set of ISTC Banners. in *Compromising Situations: Principles in Everyday Practice*, 36. Postprints, UKIC Textile Section, London

Constantinides, I. 1993. The Case for the Second Lowest tender. Letter in *SPAB News*, **15** (4), 4

Corfield, M. 1988. Towards a Conservation Profession. in *Preprints for the UKIC 30th Anniversary Conference* (compiled by V. Todd), 4-7. London

CU and Historic Scotland, 1993. *Conservation-Restoration: The options.* London

Doré, J. 1978. The Conservation of two Eighteenth-century English Court Mantuas. *Studies in Conservation*, **23** (1), 1-14

Eastop, D. 1993. Introduction. in *Compromising Situations: Principles in Everyday Practice*, 1-5. Postprints, UKIC Textile Section, London

Finch, K. 1980. Changing Attitudes, New Developments, Full Circle. in *Conservation and Restoration of Textiles*, (ed. F. Pertegato), 82-6. CISST, Milan

Gibson, L. 1993. *The Conservation of Garment Fragments Excavated from a Leicestershire Coal Mine.* Unpublished Diploma Report, Textile Conservation Centre/Courtauld Institute of Art

Greenacre, M. 1988. Conservation in the Orient. *Conservation News*, **37** (November, 1988), 25-7

Hefford, W. 1976. Bread, Brushes and Brooms: Aspects of Tapestry Restoration in England, 1660-1760. in *Acts of the Tapestry Symposium*, (ed. A. Bennet), 65-75 (where The Lord Chamberlain's Books, L.C. 9/282, account No. 55 is quoted). The Fine Arts Museum of San Francisco, San Francisco

Hofenk de Graaf, J. 1993. Personal communication

Hughes, H. 1987. Historic Interiors in the USSR. *Conservation News*, **34** (November 1987), 12-14

Jones, M. (ed) 1990. *Fake? The Art of Deception*. The British Museum, London

Lister, A.M. 1994. Treatment Report, TCC 1603. Unpublished documentation report, Textile Conservation Centre

NZPCG, 1991. *Code of Ethics*. The New Zealand Professional Conservators' Group, Wellington

Orlofsky, P. and Trupin, D.L. 1993. The Role of Connoisseurship in Determining the Textile Conservator's Treatment Options. *Journal of American Institute for Conservation*, **32**, 109-18

Rollins, A. 1992. *The Conservation and Reconstruction of an Eighteenth-century Sack Backed Dress*, Unpublished Diploma Report, Textile Conservation Centre/Courtauld Institute of Art

Wedge, T. 1993. Consideration of Protocol when Treating Ceremonial Textiles. in *Compromising Situations: Principles in Everyday Practice*, 38-9. Postprints, UKIC Textile Section, London

Plate 1 (above) *Anthony and Cleopatra*, seventeenth-century Brussels tapestry, showing the 'restored' leg in a contrasting orange colour.
Reproduced by kind permission of the Worshipful Company of Goldsmiths

Plate 7 (right)   *Children at Play*, seventeenth-century English tapestry, holed area after treatment (see Plate 6)

Plate 2   Silk shawl before treatment. Cobbled repairs within fringe heading. Reproduced by kind permission of the private owner

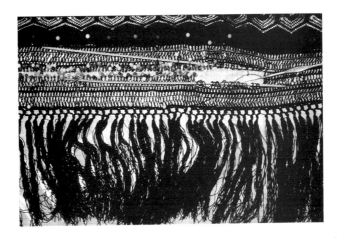

Plate 3   Silk shawl, stitched repairs removed and knitted structure being reintroduced

Plate 4   Silk shawl, fringe heading following restoration

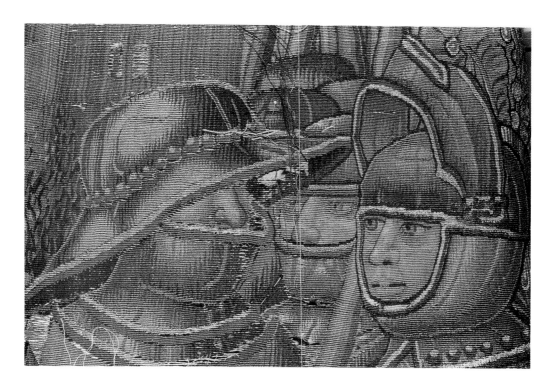

Plate 5 *Triumph of Fortitude*, 1525 Brussels tapestry. Details of conservation in progress, left side before and right side after treatment. Reproduced by kind permission of the Board of Trustees of the National Museums and Galleries on Merseyside (Walker Art Gallery)

Plate 6 *Children at Play*, detail of boy satyr climbing tree, seventeenth-century English tapestry, before treatment with patched holes. Reproduced by kind permission of The National Trust

118

Plate 8   ISTC banner, fragmented area prior to insertion of painted patch. The new silk, which can be seen lying behind, is that of the full support given to the whole banner. Reproduced by kind permission of Glasgow Museum

Plate 9   ISTC banner, fragmented area following insertion of painted patch

Plate 10   Two garment fragments (back panels) before treatment

Plate 11   Garment fragments after treatment (cleaning and stitched support) and mounted for display on padded torso

Plate 12   Eighteenth-century dress before treatment, with later alterations made for fancy dress. Reproduced by kind permission of Leicester Museums and Records Service

Plate 13   Full scale white toile of the much altered dress, showing additions required (in dark fabric) to reconstruct its original eighteenth-century cut

TCC 1581/2
AFTER

Plate 14 The dress after treatment, which included the removal of alterations. New printed fabric was added to replace missing areas of the original pattern-woven silk; the new fabric can be seen at the left bodice and upper skirt, where it allowed the original cut to be reconstructed.

THE TREATMENT OF AN UPRIGHT GRAND PIANOFORTE *C*.1808

Timothy Hayes
Museum of London, London Wall, London EC2Y 5HN

INTRODUCTION

The upright grand pianoforte is an unusual example of a rare form of English piano-building. Essentially a grand piano in an upright position, there are very few technical and acoustic differences between this early nineteenth-century instrument and its horizontal contempories (Harding 1978; Good 1982). The keyboard is of seventy-three notes, CC-c and is trichord strung throughout. The instrument was offered on loan to the London Museum by King George V1 in 1938. It is not known if the pianoforte was ever displayed at that date, or in exactly what structural condition the object was lent. A retired member of the museum's staff, whose career predates that of the loan, recollects that the instrument was never put on display due to the deteriorated appearance of the object. A publication containing a black and white photograph of the instrument, taken approximately ten years before the acceptance of the loan, confirms part of this testimony. The pianoforte remained in storage for a further fifty-five years before it was assessed for treatment and eventual display.

In January 1992, a structural condition report, commissioned by the Royal Collection, was undertaken. Each of the pianoforte's component parts were individually examined and recorded. Two external experts in the field of early keyboard instruments examined the instrumental element, which lead to a most notable finding: that the instrument's action had remained in a rare state of preservation. In fact, the instrument had survived without any apparent alteration or replacement of component parts since its manufacture in 1808.

HISTORY

The upright grand pianoforte, encased in a gothic revival cabinet, was supplied to the Prince of Wales for his London residence at Carlton House and invoiced as follows on 15 August 1808 (Royal Collection, RA 29011):

> A curious fine toned Six Octave Upright Grand Piano Forte/in black Ebony Case, designed from the antique/Supported by four Strong Gothic Columns; Moulding/and Cornice formed of the best Workmanship/Carving & Gilding the Columns, Moulding and/Cornice; in Burnish and Mat Gold,/Ivory Balls Rosets & Orniments for do/Japanning the Inside of the Case a Royal Crimson/Fine Locks Water Gilt and Hinges/Silk Curtains made full with gathered Heads for do/An Elegant Bookcase Complete in all respects to/Match the Piano Forte .... £ 680 0s 0d.

The pianoforte formed part of the decorative furnishings to the Gothic library created in the basement storey of Carlton House in 1806 (Catalogue 1991). It is inscribed on the nameboard: 'R. Jones. UPRIGHT GRAND & SQUARE Piano Forte Maker, To His Royal Highness the Prince of Wales, No. 11, Golden Square, London 1808'.

A surviving maintenance record of the pianoforte describes it being sent for tuning from Carlton House on 20 November 1820, to 'Mr Stumff No.44 Great Portland Street, Marylebone' (Royal Collection, Benjamin Jutsham's Delivery Book, Vol III, p. 12). By the time Carlton House was demolished in 1827, the pianoforte had been transferred to Royal Lodge. A paper label, pasted onto the back of the instrument, bears the inscription 'GvR, Buckingham Palace, LCD', suggesting another movement approximately one hundred years later.

MATERIAL COMPOSITION AND CONDITION

Assembled, the pianoforte measures: height 276cm x width 114cm x depth 56cm. Composed of two main structural elements, the base and cased instrument, the object can be further subdivided by removing the mirrored doors, crenellated cornice, fall boards, nameboard, rear panel and action. Once disassembled, each component part can be easily examined and its structural composition and condition identified. Essentially, the instrument is encased within an oak carcase, veneered with Indian ebony. Applied to this ground are various decorative devices including: sections of ebony moulding, brass inlays, panels of carved and gilt gothic tracery, and inlaid ivory motifs.

The material composition of the instrument conforms with other keyboard instruments of the period. It has limewood keys, with ivory covered naturals and ebony sharps. The action, supported within a mahogany framework, is fitted with a number of mechanical components (hammers, dampers, stickers, etc.) fabricated from various organic and inorganic materials. The soundboard is of spruce, held within a hardwood framework and braced by various woods. The yoke of the frame is stamped by the maker: R.JONES & Co. 855. The instrument is trichord strung throughout, with the lowest four courses of overspun brass, passing over the short bridge. The remaining fifty-two courses are of plain iron wire and pass over the long bridge. Three fabric tapes dampen the ends of the stringing, between frame and bridge (Plate 1).

The structural condition of the object before treatment varied according to two main factors: material type and location within the instrument. The external casework has suffered considerably from the effects of differential structural movement, particularly between the oak ground, ebony veneer and applied gilded limewood carvings. Both of the external cheeks, at either end of the keyboard, have finely carved tracery panels which have split across their vulnerable short-grain sections and become loose or detached. Dehydration of the animal glue, combined with structural deformation, has caused substantial loss of the many ebony mouldings and delicately carved gilt ornamentation that once adorned the case and cornice. Indeed the damage wrought by the effects of extreme and/or fluctuating environmental conditions has left the casework lacking many of its original decorative components. Humid environmental conditions, in conjunction with airborne pollutants, have resulted in varying levels of deterioration to the object's metal surfaces. The external surfaces of the brass and iron components were partly disfigured and/or tarnished by the products of corrosive reactions. Water gilded surfaces, which were originally protected by a tinted layer of varnish, have become significantly discoloured by the gradual accumulation of particulate deposits.

The structural condition of the instrumental section of the object, was, by contrast, in a better state of preservation. All the wooden components belonging to the keyboard action had remained unaffected by structural deformation. The original felt hammers, checks, dampers and associated leather fittings had also survived in a relatively stable condition. Only the metal components showed evidence of deterioration, with minor areas of corrosion covering the surfaces of the iron and brass fittings. The structural condition of the soundboard had deteriorated due to shrinkage of the spruce boards, causing several splits and areas of deformation. Additional movement of the surrounding framework caused excessive tensioning to the stringing resulting in the breakage of seventeen courses of brass wire (Plate 2).

It became clear that the deteriorated condition of the object's structure would demand a considerable input of conservation time and resources to achieve even a minimal level of conservation.

TREATMENT PROPOSALS

Following the findings of the structural condition report, three possible methods of treatment were selected and proposed to the Royal Collection. The options ranged from pure conservation, through a compromise, to a full restoration. Each involved different ethical implications which were fully outlined in the proposals.

(a) Minimal intervention

The first proposal, based on the principal of minimal intervention, outlined a strictly conservative approach. A programme of gentle cleaning techniques would remove most of the particulate deposits, followed by the structural stabilisation of the many damaged and deteriorated components. The keyboard action would remain in its preserved condition, while the broken sections of stringing would be removed, recorded and stored, in order to prevent any further damage to the soundboard, during subsequent movements to the object, e.g. on loan. This method of conservation would retain the object's original material, with no modern intervention to replace missing or damaged parts. The central aim of this approach would be the continued preservation of an important technical and historical musical instrument (UKIC 1983).

(b) Conservation and partial restoration

The second proposal drew a distinction between the instrumental section of the object and its decorative the casework. The treatment would follow the principle outlined in proposal (a) for the instrumental section, but would undertake a programme of restoration for the missing elements of casework. This would include the more extensive areas of incomplete decoration, which visually disrupted the overall design and appearance of the object:

(i)   large sections of missing tracery ornament;
(ii)   missing sections of veneer and moulding;
(iii)   missing sections of brass inlay.

The missing components would only be reproduced where an existing example survived and could be scrupulously copied. The aim of this proposal was to offer a more complete representation of the casework for exhibition, while preserving the unique keyboard action and soundboard in their original states.

(c) Full restoration

The third proposal was based solely on the principles of restoration and reinterpretation. An estimate was commissioned from an experienced restorer of early keyboard instruments. This outlined a method of treatment that would restore the instrument to a fully operational condition, an undertaking that would necessitate the removal and replacement of those existing components unable to withstand the pressures of instrumental usage. These included the remaining courses of wire stringing, sections of damaged framework and numerous components from the keyboard action. Other sections of the instrument might also have required strengthening, due to the additional structural stresses applied to an operating keyboard instrument.

The casework would have been restored to the same condition as outlined in proposal (b).

The main priority of this proposal would be to return the object to a fully operational condition (Plate 3).

RECOMMENDATIONS AND SELECTION OF TREATMENT

The Museum of London recommended the second proposal as one which would simultaneously preserve the essence of the object, namely the instrumental components, whilst undertaking a sympathetic restoration of the decorative casework. The combination of conservation and restoration would allow the important documentary value of the object to be retained and not irretrievably lost through excessive replacement. The casework would be returned to a more complete state.

This project is set against a background of contemporary ethical debate and discussion (Karp 1985; Arnold-Foster and La Rue 1993) and there are several issues which are particularly pertinent to the treatment of this object.

1. At the current time, the status of musical instruments within the museum environment seems to be unclear. That is to say, should the instrument be left as an exhibit *per se*, or should it be played in order to provide additional acoustic information in the form of musical recitals?

2. It has been claimed that an instrument with a mechanism as complex as a piano may suffer from continued use and may not, after many years of gradual deterioration, produce a sound faithful to its original acoustic identity. Would it not, in this case, be preferable to construct a reproduction instrument employing new materials but original techniques in order to obtain an accurate impression of how the instrument sounded in its original condition?

3. It is inevitable that any instrument used for recitals will suffer a degree of wear and tear to various parts of the mechanism. In this case, any replacement or reparation will further damage the integrity of the piano, and eventually the mechanism may become unrecognisable from the instrument we see today. Surely this is undesirable?

4. A parallel can be drawn between the piano and a clock kept running for exhibition purposes. Would it be justifiable, or even desirable, to continually replace worn parts of the movement in order that the clock be seen to be working until such time as few or no original parts remain?

5. The piano is a unique example of an upright grand pianoforte with an original mechanism. As it is of such rarity, it should be preserved in its current state to enable future examination, rather than alter its mechanism until it resembles other pianofortes of its type. Surely, it is not worth irretrievably losing such rare original workmanship for the sake of hearing the piano.

Upon receipt of the Museum of London report and estimate for the restoration of the instrument's mechanism, the Royal Collection advised the Museum that they would be in favour of a full restoration of both the casework and the instrumental section (proposal c) and indeed that 'it would convey a most misleading impression ... to show it in any other way'. However, given the prohibitive time constraints and budgetary limitations, enforced by the preparations for *London - World City* exhibition in Essen (Fox 1992), the restoration of the pianoforte preferred by the Royal Collection could not be undertaken. In the five months available it was possible to fully implement the second proposal (a compromise between conservation and restoration) with the instrumental mechanism conserved but unaltered and the casework restored to a more complete condition.

CONCLUSION

The project involved a discussion of the ethical considerations which lie at the very heart of the title of this conference: *Restoration - is it acceptable?* It is axiomatic that every object should be treated on its own merits and according to its individual condition and history. Conservation is fundamental to the preservation of our national heritage if vital historical objects are not to be irretrievably lost. Restoration is only an option where the integrity of the object cannot be endangered. It therefore, follows that the 1808 Jones upright grand pianoforte should remain in its current condition and undergo no further restoration (Plate 4).

The instrument was illustrated 'exclusively' in a colour engraving in *Records of Fashion* for 1808. The accompanying text recorded a visit to Mr Jones's premises in Golden Square: 'From a great number of our first amateurs, whose curiosity led them to see and try the elegant upright grand piano ... made for his Royal Highness. The beauty of the workmanship, but above all, the rich quality of tone it possesses, drew forth the most rapturous exclamations, and must have proved the highest gratification to Mr Jones, who has spared neither labor or expense, to produce an instrument which might not be excelled, either for beauty or tone.'

ACKNOWLEDGEMENTS

I would like to thank the following Museum of London staff for their assistance during the research and treatment of the upright grand pianoforte: Dr Celina Fox, The Museum of London Exhibition Coordinator for *London - World City*; Robert Payton, Senior Applied Arts Conservator, for advice and encouragement; Francis Brodie, Applied Arts Conservator, for assistance with the conservation of the numerous metal components; Barbara Heiberger, Senior Textile Conservator, for conserving the damask textile panel; and Lyndsey Morgan, Applied Arts Intern, without whose assistance during the project, the object would not have been completed in time for the exhibition. I would also particularly like to thank Hugh Roberts, Deputy Surveyor of The Queen's Works of Art, for researching the object's royal history.

Finally, I wish to thank Lisa Hayes, for her editorial assistance and encouragement with this paper.

REFERENCES

Arnold-Foster, K. and La Rue, H. 1993. *Care and Use of Collections*, 22-33. London

Catalogue, 1991. *Carlton House, The Past Glories of George IV's Palace.* The Queen's Gallery, Buckingham Palace, London

Fox, C. 1992. *London-World City 1800 - 1840.* Yale

Good, E.M. 1982. *Giraffes, Black Dragons, and Other Pianos. A Technological History from Cristofori to the Modern Concert Grand.* Stanford

Harding, R.E.M. 1978. *The Piano Forte. Its History traced to the Great Exhibition of 1851.* London

Karp, C. 1985. Musical Instruments in Museums. *International Journal of Museum Management and Curatorship*, **4** (2), 179-82

UKIC, 1983. *Guidance for Conservation Practice*

Plate 1   The upright grand pianoforte: section of the bass end showing the condition of the decorative casework before treatment

Plate 2   Section of the action showing the condition of the hammers and stickers before treatment

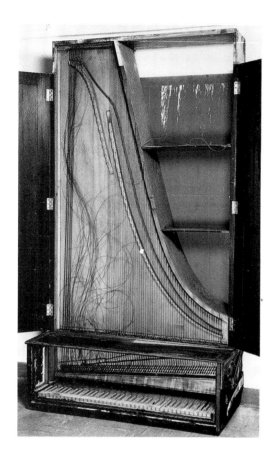

Plate 3   Condition of the instrument before treatment

Plate 4   The upright grand pianoforte
after treatment

THE RESTORATION OF VEHICLES FOR USE IN RESEARCH, EXHIBITION, AND DEMONSTRATION

P.R. Mann

Formerly at The Science Museum, Exhibition Road, South Kensington, London SW7 2DD

The key word in the title of this paper is the word 'use'. Objects are acquired to be used: they are acquired not simply for the sake of having them about the place, but so that they may be put to some useful purpose, if not immediately, then at some time in the not too distant future. All museums use objects, generally through exhibition or research. But it is in technical museums, and vehicular collections in particular, that objects are at their most utilitarian. For these museums also section objects, and demonstrate objects in motion. This utilitarian view of objects has led to the treatment of objects in technical museums in a very non-conservative manner. In practice, the way a vehicle is to be restored depends not on some abstract notion of conservation ethics but on the use to which it is to be put.

This paper describes some of the issues involved in this process. It contrasts the utilitarian approach of the technical curator with the principled approach of the conservator, and comments on whether the former can be regarded as in any way acceptable.

Objects are used for research, for exhibition, and for demonstration; and the amount of restoration, and the degree of irreversibility of the restoration generally increase in that order. We shall consider each of these three categories of usage.

RESEARCH

Vehicles are rarely used as a source of evidence in the way in which an archaeological museum would understand.

The rhetoric of the museum profession is that objects are important pieces of material evidence which may be studied to illuminate the culture which produced them. This may perhaps be true at some stage in the future for vehicles, but at present such research as is undertaken seeks to establish a biography of the individual object so that an article, exhibition label, or catalogue entry can be written. The end result is of a purely descriptive nature. This is so because in practice technical museums do not generally seek to build up typographical collections with an abundance of evidential material. Instead they build representative collections where each object illustrates a particular stage in a sequence determined from historical literature.

The way in which objects are acquired also reinforces this tendency. A study of a known history of technology is used to identify 'gaps' in the collection which are then filled by acquisition. These acquisitions are illustrative rather than evidential. They are illustrative of a known history rather than evidence for establishing a history (Mann 1991). It is only where the historical record is weak that the objects are used as historical evidence. And then they are generally used as comparative evidence for confirming the originality of other objects rather than forensic evidence for describing the culture which produced them.

Consequently, it is difficult to provide an example where a vehicle has been used in evidence for establishing some kind of history. Perhaps this is one reason why technical museums have been less concerned about preserving evidence by careful conservation. Certainly it can be said that if in the future a reason and a methodology are developed for using vehicles in a forensic manner it will be very difficult to do so because so few vehicles survive in an unrestored condition.

A rather problematical example of a vehicle being used for research purposes, is the *Rocket* locomotive of 1829.

The remains of this locomotive have been on exhibition in the Patent Museum and then the Science Museum since 1862. As an icon of the industrial revolution it is perhaps the most important object in the Science Museum. Its significance is that it won the prize in the Rainhill Trials of 1829 to select the motive power for the Liverpool and Manchester Railway. This was the first high-speed inter-city railway and gave birth to the world-wide railway boom which transformed communications. Its technical innovation lay in the use of two cylinders with cranks set at 90°, the blast pipe for improved draught, the multi-tube fire-tube boiler with separate firebox. These set the pattern for locomotive design until the ascendancy of electric and diesel locomotives. It is the firebox which is perhaps the most interesting element and it is this which is missing from the remains.

Within the first four years of *Rocket's* short eleven-year working life several major physical rearrangements were made, and it was twice repaired after accidents. No original drawings survive which show the details of its construction at the time of the Rainhill Trials. Because of this there has always been intense speculation about the design of the firebox, with everybody dredging every last inference from the limited available evidence.

Of all the objects in the Science Museum, one might imagine that this incomplete holy relic might have been left untouched to survive as archaeological evidence. Far from it, before it came to the museum it was restored by Stephensons (the original builders) to an erroneous configuration which it could never have had in its life. Some of the anachronistic features were removed by 1900. Others were changed by 1929. In 1914, the then curator, E.A. Forward wrote a paper making proposals for restoring it to its 1836 configuration when it left service with the Liverpool and Manchester Railway. No doubt the first war prevented this from being carried out. In 1922 he prepared a specification and drawings for building the missing firebox based on the best available evidence but again this was not carried out, possibly because until 1925 he would have been busy installing the railway exhibits in the new East Block galleries and then working on the Stockton and Darlington centenary exhibition.

The problem of the design of the firebox was settled, probably for good, in 1929 as a result of two unconnected events. These were: the discovery of the Rastrick notebook (Rastrick 1829), which included a contemporary sketch of the firebox; and the desire of Henry Ford to have a working reproduction of the *Rocket* locomotive for his museum in Detroit, timed to celebrate the centenary of the Rainhill Trials. It was the Rastrick notebook which enabled a re-interpretation of the physical evidence of ironwork, rivet holes, and corrosion marks on the surviving remains of the locomotive and to make sense of the conflicting documentary evidence. Although the Rastrick notebook was the key to unlocking the problem, the surviving rivet holes showed that the sketch could not be wholly correct; the evidence of the object itself was also necessary.

It was the resources put in by Ford which spurred the necessary research. The firebox which resulted was different from Forward's best previous estimate, as shown in the model of *Rocket* built for the museum in 1909 from drawings prepared by him, and by his design of 1922. It was the building of the Ford reproduction which led to the Science Museum having a sectioned reproduction built by Stephensons in 1935, and this may well have saved the *Rocket* remains from further restoration (Reed 1970; Forward 1914 and 1922; Pendred 1929; Molyneux 1929).

EXHIBITION

Vehicles are exhibited in museums in a variety of conditions, as the following examples from the Science Museum show.

Year acquired	Age when acquired	Present state	Example
1993	1	as received; new	1992 LotusSport bicycle
1993	4	as received; sectioned	Sectioned 1989 Lexus car
1910	15	as received; decrepit	1895 Panhard car
1936	27	exhibited 30 years then restored	1909 Rolls-Royce Silver Ghost Car
1984	53	restored and sectioned	c. 1931 Albion lorry engine
1981	63	external restoration	1918 FWD lorry
1923	33	appearance change 1990	1890 C&SL tube locomotive

The criteria which are used to decide the state in which a particular vehicle will be exhibited are:

- it must do justice to the museum;
- it must do justice to the theme being portrayed;
- it must do justice to the object being exhibited.

These criteria may well be in conflict with the general museological desire not to restore objects. When the 1895 Panhard was acquired in 1910 it was exhibited without being restored. This may have been because, although it was in rather poor condition, it was still sufficiently good to represent an early motor car. It is reasonably certain that at that time there would have been little pressure from outside for the museum to feel uncomfortable about its condition.

With the increasing number of transport museums opened since the war in which vehicles tend to be shown in pristine, restored condition, there has naturally been a good deal of pressure on museums such as the Science Museum also to show vehicles in pristine condition. There is also a high degree of anthropomorphism involved in collecting and displaying vehicles; a feeling that it does not do justice to the vehicle to exhibit it in a tired, worn-out state when once it had a fine, vigorous appearance.

These pressures have been enhanced by the increasing trend towards highly polished thematic displays rather than lines of vehicles ostensibly illustrating technical progress. After all, if the purpose of a particular display is to show how the landed gentry lived at a particular time, it is unlikely that this will be adequately done by using a rusty car. The Marquis of Cholmondeley never did motor around in a decrepit Rolls-Royce Silver Ghost so why should the Museum pretend now that he did?

Of course, what every transport curator would dearly like to have is a collection of vehicles which are in good condition and have never been restored, but this is well-nigh impossible. One of the problems with collecting vehicles is that although they appear to be very solid, and are produced in large numbers, they live mainly out of doors and deteriorate very rapidly even before they leave service. The answer might seem to be to acquire them when new and to keep them in good condition. But institutional circumstances such as shortage of money and space may prevent this. For example, at the turn of the century when the Science Museum was deciding what sort of car to acquire to represent the emerging motor car it decided that, because of the shortage of space at the time, it could only afford to acquire one example and that would have to be as significant in its own right as was the *Rocket* locomotive. When it eventually acquired the 1895 Panhard in 1910 it was in rather poor condition, but then all the surviving early cars were (the best ones were exhibited in a display of historic cars in the 1909 Imperial International Exhibition at White City, London). Again, because of shortage of space, the Science Museum did not acquire any commercial vehicles until it acquired its Wroughton airfield site, Wiltshire, in 1980. When it was decided to build up a representative collection of buses and lorries the choice was between acquiring vehicles which already had been heavily restored by private owners or acquiring wrecks requiring restoration. It is more likely that a renaissance painting or a Georgian sideboard will survive in good condition than a fifty-year-old lorry.

Thus, when the Science Museum acquired a 1918 FWD lorry from a French field in 1981 and a *c.* 1931 Albion lorry from a Portsmouth scrap yard in 1984, the need was felt to restore both (and section the latter) before they could be regarded as plausible exhibits.

In the case of the museum's 1890 C&SL tube locomotive a decision was taken in 1990 to completely change its appearance in order to show it in the more representative livery it had carried for most of its service life rather than the unlined reddish-brown in which it had originally been supplied and to which it had been restored in 1923. At the same time its identity was changed from the erroneous No. 1 to the likeliest No. 13 (Liffen 1992).

DEMONSTRATION

All technical museums operate machines to a greater or lesser extent; they drive them by compressed air, or by electric motor, or they operate them under their own power. In writing elsewhere about this process it has been observed that they were accepting the destruction of material evidence which results from operation so that another 'more important' functional kind of evidence can be revealed to the public by the operation of the artefacts. It was concluded that what these museums were doing was acting out a more appropriate, though hitherto unexpressed, ethic for technical museums; the primary objective had become the exploitation of the artefact for the public benefit rather than the simple preservation of material evidence (Mann, 1989). In another paper, ways in which the process of degradation, which inevitably resulted, might be monitored and controlled in a more responsible manner have been described (Mann, 1990).

Before going on to look at the major reasons for the increasing severity of restoration necessary to operate vehicles, consider first the reasons why museum vehicles are operated. This diagram shows the principle reasons for operating museum vehicles arranged in order of decreasing respectability.

RESPECTABLE

1. to explain how things work
2. to show how things sounded/looked/felt
3. to show technical/social/economic/change
4. to contrast good/bad or cheap/expensive vehicles

ACCEPTABLE

5. to create interest in history,engineering/vehicles/museums
6. to inspire with the wonders/horrors of engineering
7. to create amusement/enjoyment/fun

UNACCEPTABLE

8. to publicise the museum
9. to show the museum is 'alive'
10. to show the museum is better than others
11. to bring more visitors
12. to increase income through filming/private hire
13. to attract sponsors
14. to thank sponsors
15. to impress Councillors/Trustees/Director
16. the Councillors/Trustees/Director like doing it
17. the Curator likes doing it

The first group has been labelled as respectable because they are examples of the traditional didactic role of museums, whereby objects are used to show something instructive. The second group has been labelled as acceptable because in recent years even the most traditional museums have begun to accept that the enjoyment of the visitors is at least worth considering. The third group of reasons has been labelled as unacceptable because that is how they would still be regarded by much of the museum profession. After all it is one thing to destroy museum objects for educational reasons but quite another to do it simply because the Chairman of Trustees likes doing it.

As soon as a decision is taken to run a vehicle an escalation takes place in the eternal war between the competing forces of conservation and restoration.

To get a vehicle operating in the first place it may well be necessary to do the following:

- replace missing parts
- repair worn-out/corroded parts
- replace worn-out/corroded parts.

Before it can be legally operated it may be necessary to carry out further work to satisfy regulations:

- MoT tests for road vehicles
- AID inspections for aircraft
- Lloyds inspections for ships

- boiler inspections and tests for steam vehicles on road, rail, and water. (Some early types of boiler construction are now no longer accepted and would need to be replaced by new boilers to a non-original design.)

- ultrasonic tests on wheels and axles for rolling stock to travel over BR track.

Once running it will be necessary to periodically replace what have come to be regarded as consumables. In the case of road vehicles this would include batteries, exhausts, brake and clutch linings, pivot pins, tyres.

Strictly speaking it would not normally be necessary to carry out the sort of external 'cosmetic' restoration carried out for exhibition purposes in order to demonstrate a vehicle. However, in practice it is unusual to restore a vehicle to working order without also carrying out an external restoration. Thus it might also be deemed necessary to replace paintwork and upholstery. If a vehicle carries out a substantial mileage, and particularly if it carries passengers, paintwork and upholstery may also come to be regarded as consumables.

As an example of the problems of running museum vehicles, consider the Science Museum's 1905 Rolls-Royce 10h.p. car. This is claimed to be the most original of the three surviving examples but has been repainted and re-upholstered, had new pistons, water pump, reverse gear pinion, camshaft housing and assorted pipes, and bearings and brackets replaced in order to keep it running.

As an example of the reasons why vehicles do get restored, consider the 1934 AEC Mammoth Major 8-wheel tanker which it was known at the time of its acquisition in 1983 would have to be restored. The significance of this vehicle is that it illustrates the fact that the general configuration of lorries in this country is determined almost entirely by legislation about dimensions and weights of vehicles. When the new Construction and Use Regulations came into force in 1933 it meant almost accidentally that, by adding a fourth axle to the standard three-axle heavy lorry, an extra two tons of payload could be carried. The four-axle lorry, normally referred to as an 8-wheeler, then became the mainstay of British heavy haulage until the widespread introduction of the articulated lorry in the 1960s. The AEC was the first type to be produced and the Science Museum example was the fourteenth off the production line, but it looked a complete wreck when acquired.

It was considered that no useful purpose would be served by exhibiting this vehicle in unrestored condition; it was also felt there was little to be lost, and much to be gained, by restoring it to running order so that it could be demonstrated to the public at Wroughton. Consequently it was restored to full working order. Very roughly speaking, about 85% of it is from the original vehicle, and less than 5% is new material. Clearly, almost all of what you see (the exterior finishes) is new, but the form of what you see has been greatly enhanced.

RESTORATION - IS IT ACCEPTABLE?

Some of the issues faced in restoring vehicles for use in research, exhibition, and demonstration have been described. But what is the justification for these restorations?

In the case of operating vehicles, technical museums have demonstrated quite clearly that for some vehicles they value the functional evidence revealed by operating them more than the material evidence contained within them.

I have no doubt that it is acceptable to restore some vehicles to running order and to operate them.

But in this lies the germ of a paradox. For it is often the case in a transport museum that all the vehicles have been restored to running order, but they only have resources to operate a few of them to any significant extent, or many of them to a very limited extent. If that is the case there seems little need to restore them all to running order because their legitimate didactic needs can be satisfied by running just a few of them. The problematical area therefore is, paradoxically, restoration for exhibition rather than restoration for use. Can the restoration of *all* vehicles for exhibition be justified? Consider a softer question first. Can the restoration of *any* vehicles for exhibition be justified?

I have no doubt that it is acceptable to restore some vehicles for exhibition.

There seems little intrinsically wrong with restoring a 1909 Rolls-Royce Silver-Ghost car to the pristine condition (note the vexed word 'original' is not used) in which it was used by the Marquis of Cholmondeley, if the institution concerned believes it is better to use the object in this way in an interpretive exhibition, rather than to leave it in the dilapidated state in which it was acquired, against the distant day, which may never come, when a scholar may want to use it as material evidence.

But when it comes to the question of restoring all vehicles then the restorer is on weaker ground. I could not see any useful purpose in exhibiting the 1934 AEC Mammoth Major lorry in as received condition. However, I can see a useful purpose in exhibiting the remains of the 1829 *Rocket* locomotive in its dilapidated and incomplete state as a 'holy relic' of the industrial revolution. Between these two extremes lies an infinite number and variety of *ad hoc* decisions about each individual object.

The decision as to how to treat the object will depend in part on the use to which the object is to be put. In the case of restoration for research it is scarcely an issue, in the sense that restoration is bound to reduce the evidential value for research. As it happens, in practice vehicles are rarely used as material evidence for research of the forensic type in which an archaeological museum might indulge. Studying vehicles prompts many questions which are usually then answered from other sources. For example, when a veteran car is dated it is usually by reference to the manufacturer's records. It is a moot point as to whether the lack of original vehicles has led to this state of affairs, or whether the lack of a need to preserve material evidence has led to the wholesale restoration of vehicles. Having said that, it is a universal instinct that, other things being equal, all curators and collectors would prefer to have unrestored and hence more 'original' vehicles even if there is no possibility of using them as material evidence.

CONCLUSION

Although vehicles are rarely used as material evidence in research, curators and collectors would prefer to have unrestored and 'original' vehicles. However, there are legitimate reasons for restoring some vehicles for exhibition purposes, and restoring some vehicles to working order for demonstration purposes. The difficult decisions for vehicle curators are which vehicles to restore, how many vehicles to restore, and how to record, monitor, and control the degradation and loss of originality which occurs.

Logic and twenty years of experience of technical museums has resulted in this utilitarian and pragmatic view of the role of museum objects. If part of the role of the conservator is to act as a conservative restraining influence on over-zealous restoration, then it is equally part of the role of the curator to say how objects should be restored appropriately for their use for the benefit of the public.

BIBLIOGRAPHY

Forward, E.A. 1914. 'The Rocket'. Unpublished notes in Science Museum Technical File 1862-5

Forward, E.A. 1922. 'Notes on a Re-constructed Firebox for the *Rocket* Locomotive'. Unpublished notes in Science Museum Technical File 1862-5, 17 August 1922

Liffen, J. 1992. Locomotive from first Tube Railway. in *Making of the Modern World - Milestones of Science and Technology*, (ed. N Cossons), 120-1. London

Mann, P. R. 1989. Working Exhibits and the Destruction of Evidence in the Science Museum. *The International Journal of Museum Management and Curatorship*, **8**, 369-87

Mann, P. R. 1990. The Implications of using Museum Vehicles. in *The Way Ahead*. Papers from the First World Forum of Motor Museums held at the National Motor Museum, Beaulieu, 6-10 November 1898, (ed. D. Zeuner), 22-34. World Forum of Motor Museums, Beaulieu

Mann, P.R. 1991. Making the Wheels go round - Why do we collect Engines, Exhibit them in power halls, and Operate them? Paper read at Ironbridge Institute/SICG seminar, Science Museum, 5 Nov. 1990. Condensed version published *SICG Newsletter* Spring 1991

Molyneux, A.H. 1929. 'Memorandum on the Replica of the *Rocket* constructed by Robert Stephenson & Co Ltd, Darlington, England, 1929 For Henry Ford Esq'. Unpublished volume in Science Museum Technical file 1862-5. Molyneux was Stephenson's chief draughtsman

Pendred, L. 1929. The *Rocket*. *The Engineer*, 31 May 1929, 592-5

Rastrick, J.U. 1829. Untitled manuscript notebook known as 'Rastrick's Rainhill Notebook, 1829', Science Museum Inv No 1945-108. Rastrick was an engineer commissioned by the Liverpool and Manchester Railway to advise on motive power and he became one of the judges at the Rainhill Trials. The notebook contains descriptions, dimensions, sketches, performance details of all the competitors at the Trials.

Reed, B. 1970. *Loco Profile No. 7 - The Rocket*. Windsor

PUTTING THINGS IN CONTEXT
THE ETHICS OF WORKING COLLECTIONS

Robert Child

Department of Conservation, National Museum of Wales, Cathays Park, Cardiff CF1 3NP

INTRODUCTION

The Museums Association in its first Journal of 1900 states: 'Museums have many forms, just because art and nature produce many forms and the human intellect gives varied forms to its many ideas. Consequently Museums are various, embracing art, nature and humanity.' (Museums Association Journal 1900)

It goes on to describe eight categories of museum: the National, the Artistic, the Scientific, the Scholastic, the Educational, the Technological, the Personal and the Municipal. However, despite the spread of interests covered by these institutions they all have developed similar aims and objects, covered by their charters and ethical codes. Typical of these codes of ethics is the American Association Code of Ethics 1978 which states: 'Museums make their unique contribution to the public by collecting, preserving and interpreting the things of the world.'

It is in the word 'interpreting' that a conflict with preservation has arisen. Interpreting means - to bring out the meaning of, to explain, to elucidate. In the museum context this can cover such areas as pure research, for instance in taxonomic classification of natural history specimens, or the identification of pigments in works of art. It will also necessarily include the use of specimens by researchers wishing to study their areas of interest, and the display of objects to the general public for the wider dissemination of knowledge.

CONSERVATION ETHICS

An ethical base for the conservation and restoration of works of art has been with us for many centuries, probably since Ptolemy built his 'Temple of the Muses' in AD 2 at Alexandria and gave museums their name. However it is only in the last few hundred years that the need for a ethical base has been essential to combat the rise in faking, fraud and falsification of works of art as their desirability, and thus value, increased in response to a greater demand. (Irresponsible management of collections by researchers, curators and collectors who have had no professional respect for the objects in their care, has also led to the development of ethical constraints.)

In this century many of the generally accepted restoration ethics have been based on a mixture of fashion and the need to validate antiquities to a date and maker. Thus, degraded varnish is removed from an oil painting for aesthetic reasons and to elicit further information on colour, technique, etc., to help identify the artist, while antique furniture has its degraded surfaces preserved as the patination of age helps to differentiate the original from a modern copy.

The post-war period has seen a rapid advance in scientifically-based conservation techniques. A better understanding of the causes of degradation and of the reaction of materials to their environment has resulted in improved methods for long-term preservation. However, there is still the problem that most conservation research is directed at the composition of objects and not their preservation. Gael de Guichen bemoans the fact that 90% of conservation scientists have no conservation training, and he proposes post-graduate training for scientists wishing to work in the conservation field (de Guichen 1991). Most current conservation ethics and codes of practice from the major institutes of conservation - UKIC, AIC, IIC, ICOM Conservation Committee, etc, were formulated in the 1970s and 80s when the first generation of conservator graduates began to establish themselves in the museum community. The statements of ethics showed a marked similarity to each other in the purity of their purpose in maintaining the 'integrity' of an historical or artistic work. Unfortunately, in those heady days it was thought (or hoped, or dreamed) that a code of ethics for the preservation of objects should be applicable to all situations for it to have any viability. The constraints that some conservators put on the use of objects in museums alienated them from the custodians (the curatorial staff) and, in many cases, the public who complained of lack of access to the collections, refusal of loans, difficult viewing conditions, etc.

Conservation staff and associated conservation scientists increasingly do not work with collections or exhibitions, except in smaller museums where there is usually a more co-operative spirit among staff than exists in large institutions. Conservators conserve individual objects in workplaces that may be remote from the collection. Preventive conservation measures may often be carried out by junior curatorial staff who will change thermohygrograph papers, inspect insect traps, and measure light and UV levels. Even the condition reporting of objects and collections is often done on a 'consultancy' philosophy whereby a sample selection is examined in a statistical manner and a report produced on the state of the museum storage. Some conservators even feel their status is enhanced by this increasingly remote and hands-off approach to the items in their care. They have become consultants, advisers and, occasionally, menders and repairers. One major reason why this may be so is the restrictions imposed by a slavish obedience to current conservation ethics. It leaves the conservator with little practical work to do. Most conservators are not equipped or trained to do detailed examinations of objects, are nervous about extensive 'conservation versus restoration' decisions, and are happiest hiding behind the ethics so that they are left with preventive conservation and minimal practical interference. Worst of all, unlike their old-time counterparts, they often have no traditional craft skills to make replicas or copies, or to carry out traditional repairs, and often can have little idea of the conditions in which the original items were made and used.

USED AND WORKING COLLECTIONS

If one accepts any one of the current conservation guidelines on ethics, published by the different conservation bodies, the use of an object is severely curtailed, if not forbidden. The idea of infinite preservation is axiomatically only potentially achievable by removing it from the hands and gaze of the staff and public. Anything less is a cynical but necessary compromise. For example:

- 50 lux (5ft candles) is a compromise between the viewer seeing the object and the minimising of damage by light.
- 20°C (68°F) is for the comfort of visitors not for the preservation of materials.
- 50% RH is to allow handling in comfort as lower RHs can embrittle organic materials.

Conservation treatments are supposed to be undertaken only under the most stringent of precautions: those of,

- professionalism of the conservator having proven competence;
- minimum intervention;
- reversibility of processes;
- full documentation.

140

It is now well accepted that in most conservation treatments, few if any of these criteria can be fully met. Most conservators are required to treat objects beyond their specialism. Requirements of safety, handleability and use means that minimum intervention is not possible and the concept of reversibility has been shown to be a chimera. Even full documentation is a subjective issue on which many conservators are divided.

Pragmatically, ethical considerations are seen not as practical guidelines but as ideals which, while not achievable, should be striven for. They were put into place not to straitjacket the curator or designer but to provide them with sensible objectives.

'Working' collections are commonly thought to mean machines that are run, such as steam-engines, clocks and water mills. However, it is more useful and accurate to think of a working item as one set in a contextual surrounding and thus more at risk from deterioration. There are of course sliding scales of contextual use to make an object's interpretation understandable or vivid. The unglazing of a picture, chairs and tables in open room settings, 'touch and feel' sculpture galleries are all examples of working exhibits made more available to the viewer and toucher. The increased benefit to the public - which is often seen as an egalitarian move, allowing them the same privileges of close contact as the elite researchers - is undeniable. If it is thought acceptable, as more private owners and an increasing number of museum directors, curators and designers do, then conservators must rethink their fundamental ethical viewpoints without retreating from their basic precepts of integrity and preservation. A possible way forward is to view museum collections, not as individual items like a picture on a wall or a Roman artefact in a glass case, but as assemblages in a contextual scene.

The maximum historic and artistic value of an object is only realised when the context of that object in its natural setting is fully exploited. The inter-relationship of objects and people provides a more rounded explanation of an event or period in history or art than contemplation of the object in a cultural vacuum. As a result, individual items in a display may become less important (and even disposable) than the complete system. An individual cog in an eighteenth-century waterwheel can be sacrificed for gain, because the waterwheel works and fulfils its original function and the craft survives in maintaining and repairing it. The historic house can minimise damage and wear on its contents by suitable housekeeping, while allowing a degree of public access. Sometimes current dubious restoration practices will be shown up as fallacious such as the ruinous restoration of a clock movement purely to make it 'work'. The small gain in having the hands rotate (which can also be done with a replacement movement) must be balanced against the loss of original parts, wear patterns, etc.

Many curators, collectors, conservators and restorers will have to start asking some fundamental and difficult questions as to the reason behind their ethical practices. Some will hide behind custom and practice, minimum intervention, established ethics etc. It would be nice to hope, however, that a greater and more thoughtful dialogue on the value of objects to the museum can be considered. The following is a personal viewpoint on the basic thought processes necessary before an object is conserved, repaired or restored.

ETHICAL GUIDELINES FOR WORKING AND USED COLLECTIONS

1.   What is the greatest value of this object to the museum?
       e.g. uniqueness, age, commercial value, context, educational value

2.   Is that value likely to change over time?
       e.g. by increasing value, deterioration, increasing rarity, etc.

3.   What conservation, restoration or repair, etc, will enhance the above answers?
       e.g. preservation, restricted access, limited use, inevitable destruction, etc.

4.   What will be the long-term benefit to the museum from the above procedure?
      e.g. long-term existence, extended working life, higher educational profile, aesthetic
      improvements, closer to original condition/appearance, etc.

5.   Does the museum have the expertise to carry out the work, the finances to pay for it, the
      facilities to house the work, and the ability to maintain the completed object.

CONCLUSION

The statements of ethics currently in use have served the conservation community well over the last
two decades. However, the increased use of museums, galleries and historic houses and a desire for
realism in the displays and exhibits has changed the public's attitude to the accessibility of objects by
demanding that they be more 'user-friendly'. The concomitant risk of increased damage, wear, and
general deterioration is offset by the greater availability and enjoyment of the objects by a larger
number of people.
      The preservation of the object is not necessarily the overwhelming priority of the museum and
its staff. The preservation of the historical, cultural, spiritual and artistic context in which the object
was realised is often more important, and the maintenance of the skills and expertise that constricted,
repaired, and maintained the object ensures the continuity of the arts and crafts that gave us our
cultural heritage.

BIBLIOGRAPHY

Ashley-Smith, J. 1986. Individual responsibility in Ethical Conservation. Abstract in *New Directives
      in Paper Conservation*, p.D34. Institute of   Paper Conservation Conference at Oxford

Beeton, I. 1861. *Book of Household Management*. London

Child, R.E. 1988. Ethics in Conservation of Social History Material. *Preprints for the UKIC 30th
      Anniversary Conference* (compiled by V. Todd), 8-9. London

Child, R.E. 1993. Ethics. in *Social History in Museums: A Handbook for Professionals*, 297-302.
      London

Corfield, M. 1988. The Re-shaping of Archaeological Metal Objects: some ethical considerations.
      Antiquity, **62**, 261-5

Corfield, M. 1988. Towards a Conservation Profession. *Preprints for the UKIC 30th Anniversary
      Conference*, (compiled by V. Todd), 4-7. London

de Guichen, G. 1991. Scientists and the Preservation of Cultural Heritage. in *Science, Technology
      and European Cultural Heritage*, (eds. N.S. Baer, C. Sabbioni and A.I. Sors), 17-26. London

Frost, M. 1980. Care and Conservation of Machinery. *J.Assoc. of Manitoba Museums,
      Saskatchewan Museum Quarterly* **7** (8), 11-18

Glasse, H. 1760. *The Servants Directory and Housekeepers' Companion*. London

Harding, K. 1976. *A code of Ethics for Restorers in Antiquarian Horology*. K. Harding, London

Hayward, A.J. 1988. *Towards a Code of Practice for Working Exhibits*, Dissertation for M.Sc. (Museum Studies), University of Leicester

Hedley, G. 1986. Cleaning and Meaning: the Ravished Image Reviewed. *The Conservator*, **10,** 2-6

Hooper-Greenhill, E. 1992. *Museums and the Shaping of Knowledge*. London

International Council of Museums: Committee for Conservation, 1978. *The Conservator-Restorer: A Definition of the Profession*

Monger, G. 1988. Conservation or Restoration. *The International Journal of Museum Management and Curatorship*, **7,** 375-80

Museums Association, 1900 *The Museums Association and its Journal*, 3-6. London

Museums and Galleries Commission, 1993. Standards in the Museum Care of Industrial and Social History Collections: Larger and Working Objects (4th Consultation Draft). London

Scottish Conservation Directory, 1985-86. *What is Conservation?*, 8. Scottish Development Agency and Conservation Bureau, Edinburgh.

Standing commission on Museums and Galleries, 1980. *Conservation*. (Report by a Working Party) London

Standing Commission on Museums and Galleries, 1971. *The Preservation of Technological Material*, London

United Kingdom Institute for Conservation, 1984. *Guidance for Conservation Practice*. London

Walden, S. 1985. *The Ravished Image*. London

Wallace, G. 1988. Conservation Ethics and Management within a private Company. *Preprints for the UKIC 30th Anniversary Conference* (compiled by V. Todd), 10-14. London

FILLING LACUNAE IN FLORENTINE MOSAIC AND TESSERA MOSAIC: REFLECTIONS AND PROPOSALS

Annamaria Giusti

Opificio delle Pietre Dure, via degli Altani, 78-50121 Firenze, Italy

In Italy, the body of theory which guides (or is supposed to guide) the restoration of works of art rests substantially on the principles laid down by Cesare Brandi. He was the inspiration behind the Restoration Charter of 1972, the official document of the Ministry of Culture, which laid down guidelines for state institutions engaged in restoring and safeguarding the national artistic patrimony. Brandi was, for many years, Director of the Central Institute for Restoration in Rome; he was at the same time active as an art historian and theoretician, and to him belongs the credit for having established art restoration as a 'discipline', steering it away from arbitrary and subjective criteria (Brandi 1963).

It is, nevertheless, a discipline bound to change, and could not be otherwise, given that restoration is always the expression of a particular cultural moment, and is destined to evolve in an organic relationship with historical consciousness. In the 1930s and 1940s, when Brandi was developing ideas, 'repristination' was still the dominant ideal of restorers, an ideal which derived its *raison d'être* from late nineteenth-century Romantic historicism, and which led to subjective and arbitrary mistreatment of works of art by restorers, even in quite recent times. Respect for the integrity of a work of art as it has come down to us through the ages was the revolutionary foundation of Brandi's theories, which did not, however, utterly renounce the search for possible solutions for the treatment of lacunae. Such treatment he considered legitimate where it did not prejudice the future of the work nor alter its essence. Even the rigorous principles of Brandi leave room for a variety of specific solutions adapted to the intrinsic nature and condition of works of art.

Brandi's writings, and the Restoration Charter itself, do not indeed forbid the filling of lacunae in paintings, in sculptures or in architecture. These are, of course, the canonical 'major arts', consecrated as such by the thinkers of the Renaissance, and after the 'all-inclusive' interests of Positivism in its various artistic guises, the three arts were replaced at the summit of the hierarchy proposed by the philosophical movement of aesthetic Idealism, the context within which Brandi developed his ideas.

In recent times there has been a revaluation of multiple artistic forms, and a revival of a 'culture of materials'. For this reason, restorers have turned their attention to the applied arts, the extreme variety of which (in typology, materials and function) has given rise to a series of problems, many of which are quite new from the technical and methodological points of view.

Restorers have thought a good deal about these problems at the Opificio delle Pietre Dure in Florence, a state institute specialising in art restoration, which, perhaps because it was originally the artistic workshop of the Tuscan Grand-ducal court, is today particularly involved in the decorative arts. Florentine Mosaic was in former times the pride and joy of the Grand-ducal workshop, and superb examples of it are today to be found in the great museums of the world. It is composed of precious marbles, or more often of *pietre dure*, sawn by hand into complex shapes and fitted together to form figurative compositions. Florentine Mosaic was intended to last for centuries; damage occurs only as the result of accidents, or of wear and tear which, in the case of such precious objects, was generally avoided.

It was unfortunate therefore that, in this respect, a large table inlaid with polychrome marbles, preserved in the Ducal Palace of Mantua was traversed by a deep fracture and also worn away at the edges. Some of the archaeological marbles set into the white marble ground had been lost, although sufficient remained to give certain indications of the design and materials of the missing portions. In an earlier attempt at restoration, the lacunae had been crudely filled with black stucco and with a coloured gesso, now discoloured. It was decided to remove these inadequate or deteriorated additions, and to fill the lacunae using only original materials and techniques, following a precise design derived from the surviving portions and avoiding arbitrary choices (Giusti *et al* 1986). It was considered that in cases of this kind it is legitimate to make 'faithful' additions, given that the material constituting the work of art is subordinated to the total image representing the artist's intention. In other words, the material contributes to the image but is not an integral and irreplaceable part of it, as would be the case of a painting or sculpture. The production of Florentine Mosaic was indeed a collaborative venture; the design of the *modello* was entrusted to a 'creative' artist (usually a painter, sculptor or architect), while the translation of the *modello* into the finished object was carried out by skilled stone workers. In filling the lacunae in a mosaic, the unrepeatable role of the creative artist is not usurped, but rather the craftsman's task of translating the design into practice is undertaken.

Wherever it is possible to make use of the traditional skills (skills which are today threatened with extinction, even at the Opificio, because of the scarcity of young specialists), we consider that restoring Florentine Mosaic with the original materials and techniques is the ideal method, the one most suitable for giving back to these works of art their decorative value and material worth (the two being closely connected) in the way that was originally conceived by their makers. Restorers do not, however, abandon their responsibility (an unavoidable one, in modern restoration) to render their interventions both recognisable and reversible.

For this reason, the sections of newly-cut marble (Plate 1) are never set directly into the marble ground, as in the original, but into thin supporting plates screwed on to the marble ground Plate 2). These may easily be removed Plate 3). The filling of a lacuna in a mosaic must always be identifiable as such, and so a thin space, visible on close inspection, divides the new from the original portions.

During the restoration of the table, a particular problem was posed by one of the marbles needed by the restorers, a Greek breccia, known as *seme santo*, which is today only to be found archaeologically. In this one case, not having the original material to hand, use was made of an imitation, manufactured from coloured resin and marble fragments. Such a solution could be used in the restoration of Florentine Mosaic where the restorer was unable or unwilling to make use of original materials and techniques. The stone sections could be made from synthetic materials imitating marble and the shapes formed from moulds of the missing portions.

Another possibility is the use of the *scagliola technique*, which indeed was originally conceived as a less costly and less laborious alternative to stone inlay. *Scagliola* was used to fill a smallish lacuna in a vase of Florentine Mosaic from the central panel of a cabinet (Plates 4, 5). As the exact design and colouring of the missing portions was uncertain, they were made in *scagliola* so that the new work would be immediately identifiable as such (Giusti and Frizzi 1986).

The subject of tessera mosaic is a larger and more complex one, and is here restricted to a few observations. For mural mosaics composed of glass tesserae, of which there are a great many in Italy, it has been, and still is, usual to deal with lacunae by means of 'neutral' plastering. Brandi, however, regarded this practice as far too showy, and found it even less acceptable in mosaic than in fresco. His suggestion, where filling was feasible, was to make use of tesserae of coloured plaster (Brandi 1956). This method was used recently in restoring the mosaic arch in the Basilica of San Vitale in Ravenna, where tesserae, moulded out of plaster, were tinted with watercolour (Alberti and Tomeucci 1992). This would appear to be a better solution than some others which have occasionally been used, such as smooth, rough, incised or painted plaster (Cordaro 1985). Nevertheless, plaster tesserae, while they do help to fill in the surface texture, do not possess the quality of luminosity which is fundamental to vitreous mosaic and which is such an important component in our aesthetic response to it. Furthermore, the inevitable discolouration of the watercolour over the years carries the risk of eventual chromatic disharmony, even if it was avoided at the moment of restoration.

146

For all these reasons the Opificio has, in recent restorations, preferred to make use of vitreous tesserae, coloured like the originals, and cut by hand so as to avoid the unpleasing effect of flat uniformity produced by machine cutting. In order not to 'deceive' the observer, reconstruction, properly so-called, is limited to those areas where the design can be deduced with certainty on the basis of surviving portions (for example aureoles, repeated decorative motifs, geometrical or architectural elements). The reconstructed area is bordered by a row of thin transparent glass tesserae, which is easily visible from close to, but does not disturb the eye from a distance. As with Florentine Mosaic, the new tesserae are set into a special support screwed on to the plaster ground and which is easily removable.

A more difficult problem is posed by those losses where no help is given by the context, and where restorers can obviously not resort to the 're-invention' that nineteenth-century restorers went in for. In these cases, solutions have been attempted which certainly might be improved. By setting tesserae into removable supports, the lost image has been 'suggested' in abstract terms. For example, the lower legs of a figure were reconstructed with forms analogous to the originals but which are not anatomically defined (Frizzi *et al.* 1987). Larger and more evident losses are more problematical, such as the entire head of a prophet on the parapet of the upper gallery in the Baptistry of Florence. Without reconstructing the details of the face, the indefinite impression of a head was recreated with tesserae so that from a distance the bust does not appear 'decapitated', and the mosaic's luminosity remains intact Plate 6).

Such a method is clearly impractical for very large lacunae affecting entire figures. In these cases, it might be interesting to experiment with a treatment based on chromatic selection, as used in the restoration of frescoes and other paintings. By still using tesserae, which are considered most suitable for reconstructing the light-values of mosaic, a non-figurative design is created which maintains the colouration of the areas surrounding the lacuna.

Definitive solutions are hardly possible to problems of this sort; continued research will lead to more adequate means for an appreciation of the work of art from both the aesthetic and technical-historical points of view.

BIBLIOGRAPHY

Alberti, L. and Tomeucci, A. 1992. Intervento di Restauro sui Mosaici dell' arco di ingresso al Presbiterio della Basilica di San Vitale a Ravenna. Consolidamento in situ e Reintegrazione delle lacune. in *Mosaici a San Vitale e altri Restauri*, 69-78. Ravenna

Brandi, C. 1956. Nota sulla Tecniche dei Mosaici parietali in relazione al Restauro e alle Datazioni. *Bollettino dell' Istituto Centrale del Restauro*, **25-26**, 3-9

Brandi, C. 1963. *Teoria del Restauro*, Turin

Cordaro, M. 1985. Il Problema della lacune nei Mosaici. in *Conservation in Situ: Aquileia 1983*, 3 65-71. ICCROM, Rome

Frizzi, P., Giusti, A.M. and Raddi, G. 1987. Restauro di una Lunetta a Mosaico del Battistero di Firenze: Proposte tecniche e metodologiche. *OPD Restauro*. 99-106

Giusti, A.M. 1986. *Restauro del Marmo*, (ed. A.M. Giusti), 199-204. Florence

Giusti, A.M. and Frizzi, P. 1986. Summary in *OPD Restauro*, 94-6

Giusti, A.M., Frizzi, P. and Raddi, G. 1986. Summary in *OPD Restauro*, 194-204

Plate 1   A section of marble, being cut by metal wire and abrasion to fill the lacunae in Florentine Mosaic

Plate 2   Reconstruction of lacunae by means of newly-cut sections set into a support, which is to be screwed on to the ground of a table in Florentine Mosaic

Plates 4 and 5   Florentine Mosaic panel from a cabinet: before and after restoration, showing the recreation of the lost portion by means of the *scagliola* technique

Plate 6   Reconstruction, in undetermined pattern, of a thirteenth-century glass mosaic bust in the Baptistery of Florence

Plate 3   The table with the reconstructed portions ready to be inserted

THE ARMOURER'S CRAFT:
RESTORATION OR CONSERVATION?

David Edge
The Wallace Collection, Hertford House,
Manchester Square, London W1M 6BN

The debate between conservators and restorers will probably never be fully resolved, depending as it does upon protracted and convoluted arguments about semantics, usually pursued amidst a confusing maelstrom of individual (and often very strongly-held) views on the moral and ethical issues involved. There have been many different and well-reasoned approaches (Pease 1964; UKG 1973; AIC 1979; UKIC 1981; Ashley-Smith 1982; Corfield 1988) put forward to clarify the situation and establish 'codes of practice' for conservators and restorers (and all myriad combinations of the same), but inevitably everything comes down in the end to the individual. It may, therefore, be helpful when discussing the issues with a wide audience to commence with a brief outline of the approach and ideals followed by the Wallace Collection.

As far as the Armoury at the Wallace Collection is concerned, the term 'conservation' is generally taken to mean preserving existing material from further deterioration. 'Restoration', on the other hand, is usually regarded as involving the replacement of missing parts, or the re-shaping and 'repairing' of damaged areas, thereby sometimes altering an object's appearance rather more radically (usually to what is thought to have been an earlier and/or more 'authentic' stage of its existence). Inevitably there are 'grey' areas where the distinctions become blurred; cleaning a heavily dirtied or corroded surface (thereby irrevocably removing dirt and corrosion products that may have been there for centuries) is not normally regarded as restoration. Yet, strictly speaking, the conservation of such a surface could be taken to mean stabilising and preserving the dirt layers without the removal of any material whatsoever. In some cases, removal of dirt layers may return an object to its original surface finish (as far as that can be ascertained). If, however, mere cleaning is 'restoration' then virtually everyone in our profession is a 'restorer', which surely cannot be the case.

The Wallace Collection no longer acquires works of art, and neither makes nor receives loans for exhibitions; the conservation and curatorial departments are therefore fairly small. The post of 'Armourer' has both conservation and curatorial responsibility for the Armoury (some 2,500 items), as well as conservation responsibility for all other metalwork, excluding furniture mounts and bronzes. The position of Armourer is regarded as being that of a conservator rather than a restorer; most of the work involves cleaning, stabilising and display, rather than repairs and restoration. The major preoccupation at present, for example, is the removal of 1960s grease from pieces of armour, now preserved from corrosion by a layer of microcrystalline wax.[1] Occasionally, however, aesthetic and interpretative considerations may encourage, for example, the restoration of the missing finger from a gauntlet, or the replacement of a functional leather strap if it has become badly degraded; such tasks would unhesitatingly be categorised as 'restoration'.

Other British collections probably carry out more 'restoration' work from day to day than the Wallace Collection, while in the private sector most craftsmen calling themselves by the name of Armourer have traditionally been far more heavily engaged in the fabrication of replicas than in the repair and restoration of original pieces for private clients. Over the past few years this balance has been slowly changing, however, and the more competent of these craftsmen are now turning increasingly to restoration as a means of augmenting their income during the present harsh economic climate. Their clients, of course, can sometimes be museums, but can equally be dealers or collectors anxious to 'improve' an object perhaps beyond the extent that a reputable museum 'conservator' would advise. Few private sector armourers are conservation-trained; some are entirely self-taught. It is vital that the conservation profession takes a strong lead in promoting an ethical approach to restoration, since there are indications that the desire for professional status and a need to break into the 'museum market' are encouraging freelance armourers and replica-makers to observe higher standards of ethics in their work. Previously it was very much the customer's responsibility to ensure that ethical standards of restoration were adhered to, and this unfortunately could often give rise to a conflict of interest between the wishes of the client and the best interests of the object.

Many of the ethical problems that arise when the conservation or restoration needs of an object are first examined have to do with its structural integrity, and a (sometimes disastrous) preoccupation with making it appear as attractive and complete as possible to its audience, be that ourselves, other museum professionals, or the general public. Human nature has not changed much over the past few hundred years, and perhaps it is unrealistic to expect it to change now. Archaeologists still exult over their latest find, the finer and more intact the better; curators and conservators, too, enjoy working on 'wonderful' objects, and generally dread the arrival of a crateful of excavated Roman roof-nails. Although museum staff may not have the same financial interest, their attitude and appreciation of historic items is nonetheless too often worryingly similar to that of a collector delighting over his latest acquisition, or even the dealer praising his stock to a prospective client.

Too often in museums, as with private collectors, the initial view of an object is qualitative, rather than an impartial and detached assessment of its worth as an historical document, providing fragile and elusive evidence of its past history and, perhaps, its relationship with other such survivals from the past. This sometimes apparently trivial information (but valuable precisely because it is so slight and transitory that it is often overlooked or regarded as irrelevant, until too late) is preserved in an object's pre-restoration state, just as it is also present in the archaeological context of an excavated piece. Ruthlessly clean and restore it as a 'collectable' and you are destroying as much of that hidden story as the 'nighthawk' who raids archaeological sites with a metal-detector to find and later sell 'good objects', which out of context have lost much of their meaning and (to the true scholar or museum professional, at any rate) much of their real value.

This is not a new phenomenon, of course, and much has already vanished beyond recovery. That is precisely why it is so important now to educate present, and successive, generations of curators and restorers or conservators. One hopes that here the process of realisation and education is already under way; much more may need to be done in the private sector, however, not only amongst dealers and collectors but particularly with the general public, where simple ignorance can result in a daily toll of appalling loss and destruction.

The organic components of historic arms and armour are particularly fragile, and are therefore usually in an untidy, disintegrated and visually unattractive state. These, the rarest (and often most important) evidence as to wear and use, are consequently the first casualty of an object's 'improvement'. It is easier to replace a worm-riddled wooden sword-grip than to consolidate it chemically after proper analysis and identification of the wood. It is certainly easier, cheaper and more convenient to remove altogether the tattered and fraying remnants of a textile helmet-lining than to call for the services of a textile conservator. It is more practical to replace with a new wooden ramrod the wormed and splintered fragments of the whalebone original jammed for the past 200 years in the stock of a flint-lock sporting gun, just as it is more 'useful' to replace altogether the holed drumskin of the regimental drum, or to re-stock completely the scarred and cracked grip of a duelling pistol that was once used by a past owner to hammer nails!

Equally at risk from ignorance, carelessness, or greed, are the traces of decoration, the evidence of construction or use, and the original form of a damaged or corroded piece, subsequently insensitively 'cleaned' or inaccurately 'restored'. By far the most common problem encountered in the private sector (and, alas, far too often in museums as well) seems to be over-cleaning. This sometimes goes far beyond conservation, to become drastic 'restoration' of the piece to an appearance it never actually had. No matter how pretty the end result, this kind of 'restoration' is of course completely unacceptable. Unfortunately, it is often also the cheaper option, and therefore that most likely to arise from the need for a quick result, usually occasioned by commercial pressures of one sort or another. In an effort to make an object shiny and visually appealing to a customer (or museum visitor!), a common treatment is to re-surface it ruthlessly on a high-speed industrial buffer-polisher. This will not just clean and polish bare metal, but can actually physically remove it, enabling the 'restorer' to minimise or eradicate corrosion damage and remove the 'ugly' black patina of past centuries. These sometimes ancient oxide layers are often completely stable, and can of course conceal an original blued or burnished surface, or delicate gold and silver damascening, which savage buffing will remove altogether often without the operator even realising it was there in the first place. Even more robust chiselled and engraved decoration can be easily 'dragged' and blurred by such treatment.

One of the worst problems with restoration (certainly outside the museum world, although again unfortunately cases do still occur within) has once more to do with 'object improvement'. Sword blades with nicks along the edge, whether they were put there in battle or by next-door's children, are often routinely re-ground by some dealers and collectors, sometimes completely altering the shape of the blade and therefore the nature of the weapon, to the undoubted confusion of subsequent scholarship. In the nineteenth-century it was common to replace damaged blades altogether, or even worse, to change the original blade for a longer, more decorative or impressive one; unbelievably, this still happens even today. Another favourite activity, especially with dealers and collectors, is to remove the applied spikes and holes pierced in close-helmets for the attachment of funerary crests when they were placed over tombs in churches. Instead of using reversible fillers, this can often involve welding over the holes, which of course completely wrecks any useful metallurgical evidence that one might wish to extract later. Unfortunately, a sixteenth-century close-helmet 'restored' is worth considerably more than the same helmet altered for funerary use, even when such alterations may date from as long ago as the seventeenth century. Both are sought-after 'collectables', of course, but object-worship usually ensures that the funerary helmet eventually loses its identity. Church helmets were rarely photographed *in situ* anyway, making identification with a particular church (or even better, a particular tomb) very difficult. After the helmet's 'restoration', however, this task becomes virtually impossible.

Many, if not all, the abuses carried out in the name of 'restoration' owe their existence to the rising value of these historic objects on the open market. Since most museums have to compete with collectors in the same market, they too are drawn in to the same trap by the same pressures. If a museum is mounting an exhibition on the fifteenth-century Wars of the Roses, an original helmet adapted for funerary use in the seventeenth century has less impact than one in 'original' unaltered condition. No reputable museum would commission such a restoration, but if an 'improved' helmet happens to appear at auction, it would be a strong-willed curator who abstained on principle from bidding for it. In practice, of course, there is a very good chance that such restoration will go unrecognised anyway; the potential for fraud is obvious. Sometimes only X-ray examination will reveal a skilful 'repair', and how many museums routinely X-ray potential acquisitions?

The problem is compounded by nineteenth-century fakes, copies, restorations and 'assembled' pieces, often employing the same techniques, materials and craftsmanship as the originals. The worst excesses of 'restoration' today probably owe their origins to the collecting mania of nineteenth-century antiquarians, who perhaps more than at any other time in history placed object-worship before all else. Feeding this suddenly booming market were the dealers and their fakers, resulting today in collections, such as the Armoury of the Wallace Collection, containing a fascinating blend of magnificent originals and often equally magnificent nineteenth-century pastiches. Now that the value of the originals has soared even higher, it has become worthwhile to 'improve' Victorian pieces by removing or altering give-away nineteenth-century features to make them more 'authentic' and therefore more valuable, whether or not with an intention to deceive. This, again, is obviously unacceptable. Many of the fakes peddled by famous Victorians such as Samuel Pratt (Watts 1990) often did not work at all as pieces of armour, and this fact is an essential part of their interest to armour scholars, historians, and those pursuing the serious study of collectors and collecting.

The Wallace Collection, for example, contains a very attractive, but completely composite, wheel-lock pistol (Catalogue no.A1189) known to have come from the hand of Frederic Spitzer (Mann 1962), famous as a nineteenth-century Parisian dealer who employed his own craftsmen to 'improve' pieces as well as to produce outright fakes. In order to make the mis-matched lock fit the stock, half the internal lock mechanism has had to be cut away, rendering the pistol totally inoperable. Obviously it would be completely unethical to 'restore' this pistol to a useable state. If one was sufficiently concerned about its disparate elements, one could display the component parts separately, of course, since such dis-assembly would be easily reversible, but there would seem to be little point. Far better to do what has been done; display the whole pistol intact as a nineteenth-century composite confection, made for the contemporary art-collectors' market.

It is more difficult, perhaps, to decide what to do about original items re-decorated in Victorian taste. At the Wallace Collection there is no such problem; bequeathed to the nation in 1897 to commemorate its principal nineteenth-century founder, Sir Richard Wallace, it is a predominantly nineteenth-century collection displayed in a nineteenth-century manner. Within such a framework it is entirely appropriate that the Spitzer pistol should be shown as it stands. Similarly, sixteenth-century weapons that were originally plain but now are chiselled and damascened with gold and silver still fit snugly within the Wallace Collection ethos. Outside the Collection, however, market forces are left to operate for the most part unmonitored and unchecked. As with funerary helmets, a 'good' pistol is one without later alteration, so the temptation will always be there to 'restore' its original appearance. This can be dangerous, since often the original decorative scheme can only be guessed at, and in the process of filing or grinding off the later decoration there is always the strong probability that any evidence remaining as to an item's original form or surface will be lost for ever. Undoubtedly it is confusing to have to look at an object whilst mentally peeling away layers of its past history, but that is what history is all about. Surely museums should not be seeking to present a sanitised and neatly packaged view of history through a series of time capsules frozen at a particular moment in their existence? Yet that is how the vast majority of museums (and collectors) often seem to regard their collections.

Most dangerous of all are the re-conversions of objects, be they weapons, pieces of armour, or anything else that might find its way into a museum, from a present adapted state (such alterations often having been carried out during the working lifetime of a piece) to a purer and more 'original' condition, usually representing its appearance upon first being made. A typical example is the flint-lock, which first appeared in the early-seventeenth century and remained in widespread use throughout Europe until the third decade of the nineteenth century. As a method of gun ignition it was steadily replaced by the percussion system invented in about 1812, which eventually rendered it obsolete. It was, however, very easy for gunsmiths to convert pistols and long-guns to the new system, and many weapons (including some very grand and important ones) were so adapted. Until the late 1950s it was not usually worth considering re-converting these, but thereafter the value of antique guns rose faster even than property prices, and the inevitable result was a flood of 'restorations'.

Done well, these can be almost impossible to detect; part of the gun's previous history is therefore obliterated, and it gains a false (higher) value that can be reduced drastically should the re-conversion subsequently be discovered. The possibilities for deception and profit are clear. At best, no matter how careful the research or how competent the workmanship, what in essence is left is a twentieth-century restorer's impression of a seventeenth or eighteenth-century flint-lock pistol, which in a way is hardly any more useful than an accurate and well-made replica. At worst, poor re-conversion can be obtrusive and damaging to the piece, contributing little to its value and destroying its honesty and integrity as an artefact.

Poor quality, unauthentic, or irreversible repairs and replacements are bad enough, but in many ways the worst kind of restoration (or indeed, conservation) is that for which no records are kept, leaving subsequent curators and conservators completely in the dark as to what may or may not have been done to an object. Such documentation, of course, is only of use if it is readily accessible, and always associated with the item to which it relates. Should object and record become separated, the latter may just as well never have existed. Virtually all museums now require restorer/conservators, be they in-house staff or private contractors, to furnish a written (and often also a photographic) record of their work. Once again, the worst danger lies in the private sector, for a client whose percussion-converted flint-lock pistol has been skilfully, imperceptibly and expensively re-converted to its 'original' state now has a very powerful vested financial interest in 'losing' the records of that restoration.

Not every restoration is intended to deceive, of course, and it is now fashionable (at least in museums) to favour the less-than-perfect repair, enabling one to see where work has taken place. Ethically, the most dangerous restorations of all are those executed by craftsmen as skilled in their profession as their medieval or Renaissance counterparts, often using the same materials and techniques, and usually priding themselves on a 'perfect' job of re-creation. Regardless of their honest intent, or that of their clients, these are the 'restorations' that are most likely to deceive even experts when eventually they reach the art market. Similarly, the honest copies made by such craftsmen risk becoming the next generation of modern fakes. Here it is no longer enough for the craftsman to keep records for himself and his client, or even to mark the work with an unobtrusive signature which can too often be identified and obliterated by the unscrupulous. Modern technology may assist by providing the means to 'label' such work indelibly, so that scientific methods (examination by X-ray or X-ray fluorescence, for example) can identify it as modern. Ideally, perhaps, all restorers should be encouraged to lodge records of their work with museums, even posthumously if they are concerned about the confidentiality of their clients. Sadly, however, it is probable that curators and administrators of museums would not be interested in accepting, or indeed be able to accept, the extra workload. This leaves curators rummaging through the illustrations in past sale catalogues to identify a tiny fraction of the works of art that appear on the market in an unrestored state, only to disappear and re-surface later in an 'improved' condition. Photography is of crucial importance here; more illustrations in sales catalogues and within museums, as well as private collections, would do much to help identify restored pieces and trace lost provenances.

It is important to recognise, however, that restoration is not always destructive and not always unacceptable. One has only to look at modern triumphs of the restorer/conservators' craft, such as the work carried out on the eighth-century Coppergate helmet excavated in York, to feel satisfaction at how far our profession has advanced even in the last decade. Arguably, even drastic restoration can be justified in the case of very rare artefacts that would otherwise be largely incapable of interpretation in their 'original' excavated condition. In this particular case, the object and the treatment that it underwent were considered important enough to publish a comprehensive record of the analysis, conservation and reconstruction work that enabled it to be restored to its original form, revealing much of its former dramatic beauty (Tweddle 1992). Perhaps not every object in museums can be subjected to such exhaustive examination or brought to public attention by being published in this way, but our professional attitude to the exhibits in museums should ideally always be of a similarly high standard. If museum conservators are seen to be leading the field in this, their example may eventually serve as an inducement for everyone to act with similarly high professional standards and an attitude of responsibility.

NOTES

1.   *Renaissance* microcrystalline wax, available from Picreator Enterprises, Hendon, London NW4 2PN

REFERENCES

AIC, 1979. Code of Ethics and Standards of Practice

Ashley-Smith, J. 1982. The Ethics of Conservation. *The Conservator* **6**, 1-5

Corfield, M. 1988. Towards a Conservation Profession. in *Preprints for the UKIC 30th Anniversary Conference* (compiled by V. Todd), 4-7. London

Mann, J., 1962. *European Arms and Armour: Vol.I: Armour.* p. xix. Wallace Collection, London

Pease, M. 1964. I.I.C. American Group *Standards of Practice of Professional Relations for Conservators*

Tweddle, D. 1992. *The Anglian Helmet from Coppergate.* York Archaeological Trust and the Council for British Archaeology, London

UKG, 1973. Proposals for the Establishment of the British Institute for Conservation

UKIC, 1981. Guidance for Conservation Practice (N.B. currently under review)

Watts, K. 1990. Samuel Pratt and Armour Faking. in *Why Fakes Matter* (ed. M. Jones), 100-7. London

FILLING AND PAINTING OF CERAMICS FOR EXHIBITION IN THE BRITISH MUSEUM - IS IT ACCEPTABLE?

Sandra Smith

Department of Conservation, The British Museum, London WC1B 3DG

Ceramics are represented in the cultural remains of virtually all civilisations throughout history from the Neolithic period onwards. Many social needs within a culture can be answered by the potter and therefore ceramic is found representing most aspects of the society (Sparkes 1981) from the every day wares, associated with living, cooking and storage, through cups and plates associated with eating, to objects such as votive offerings and tomb figures associated with ritual/religion. Ceramics were also utilised by industry; crucibles and moulds for metal making (Needham 1980) and evaporation vessels for salt production (Sawle 1983-4) for example.

Refinements in production and manufacturing techniques and the discovery of glazes diversified their use further. Ceramics could then be valued not only for their utility, but also for their form and appearance. The nature of ceramic material means that it will be preserved under burial conditions where other materials, plant and animal products and metals for instance, may not survive. Because of this, ceramics often play a disproportionate role in the interpretation of a culture, particularly the earlier ones. They can, therefore, play an important role within a display of any culture and can represent many aspects of it (Wilson 1989a; Johnson 1993).

Within the British Museum, conservation of ceramic objects is undertaken for a variety of reasons: storage, study, publication, and exhibition. All work is carried out in the Department of Conservation by a Ceramics and Glass Section which receives objects from all of the curatorial departments.

Objects which are to be placed in **storage** are conserved following a policy of minimal intervention; work is carried out to slow down or prevent further deterioration and to make the object safe to handle. Gap-filling is limited to structural support. Emphasis is placed on passive conservation by control of the environment, selection of correct storage materials, and the use of detachable mounts or supports for the more fragile pieces (AIC 1994; UKIC 1983).

Objects which are to be conserved for **publication** or **study** may require more extensive filling to permit handling during examination, drawing etc. Fills may be required to protect broken areas, or, in the case of material such as cuneiform tablets, to link non-physical joins. Painting is tonal with no attempt to reproduce original surface finishes. These levels of filling and painting are aimed specifically at protecting the object during study.

The fourth reason for treating objects is **exhibition,** which in some cases may involve skilled restoration involving the replacement of missing areas and close colour matching. The Ceramics and Glass Section has no standard policy on the level of restoration which can be undertaken. Instead the role of restoration is considered separately for each gallery in consultation with other professional staff, especially the curators. However, the British Museum does, in fact, have most of its ceramic objects restored to some extent for display. This is due in part to the policies which the museum has towards display, but it is also a reflection of the nature of the ceramic material itself.

The British Museum is a museum of comparative cultures (Wilson 1989a; Wilson 1989b). It contains collections which cover virtually every period and civilisation within the world. Its collections range from the earliest artefacts produced by man, to contemporary material which is being made today. The artefacts therefore represent 'living' as well as 'dead' cultures.

The museum, as a place of learning, intends displays to be the starting point of further individual study, rather than a definitive exploration of a culture. The museum aims to display each culture and its relationship with others in such a way as to provoke interest, enthusiasm, and understanding from the casual visitor, whilst providing the academic community with research material.

The Museum has over six million visitors per year with a wide range of interests, intellect and age. Over 50% of the visitors are from foreign countries, and many are unable to speak or read English. Gallery space is at a premium and each object is carefully selected by the curator and designer for its relevance to the theme of the display, as well as for its own intrinsic value (British Museum 1991a). The information which accompanies each object is limited to the museum registration number, provenance, and a brief description of the object, and is only written in English.

The majority of information received by the visitor will therefore be visual, from the overall layout of the gallery, via each showcase to the individual object. The object may be in pristine condition, or it may have suffered some damage or loss. Where the loss is minimal but still allows the cultural significance of the object to be appreciated then the object can be presented to the viewer in its damaged state.

However, where the loss is more extensive the non-specialist may need assistance to understand the relevance of the object in the gallery context (Cronyn 1980). An information panel, describing the original form of the object is not an option for the majority of artefacts. A panel will take up valuable space which could be used for putting more objects on display. Furthermore, the information on a panel is of no use to visitors who are unable to read English. Detailed explanation panels in a gallery are usually restricted to 'star objects' and are used to describe objects of outstanding interest or which demonstrate a specific technique. Information about conservation is usually limited to explanations of environmental conditions in the gallery, such as, low lighting levels, or the presence of environmental monitoring equipment.

The use of replicas is not considered necessary for ceramic objects whose original form is retained even when the ceramic has to be pieced together from individual sherds. This option is usually reserved for very fragile, partially preserved artefacts, such as the birch bark bowls from Horton, Surrey (Ward, *et al.* 1992), or for crushed or corroded objects, such as the silver cups from the Hockwold Treasure (Oddy and Holmes 1992; Johns 1986) whose original form could not be visually interpreted by the viewer.

The only remaining option, apart from display panels or replicas, for an object which has been sufficiently damaged to prevent interpretation of its aesthetic or cultural value is the use of restoration (IIC-Canadian Group 1986; AIC 1994; UKIC 1983). Ideally this will involve minimum intervention from the conservator, but restitution of the missing areas may be necessary (Stransky 1978). The need for restoration may not be due to extensive damage, but rather to loss of particularly diagnostic or informative features.

Ceramic material is chemically inert within the majority of burial environments. However it is susceptible to physical damage, such as deterioration by soluble salt action, abrasion of the surfaces, and breakage. Ceramics do not form corrosion crusts, so the original surface is not obscured, except by insoluble salt deposits or marine concretions (Olive and Pearson 1975; Cronyn 1990).

The factors which allow ceramic material to survive so well in burial environments also have implications for their restoration. Many materials are difficult to restore due to their fragility, thinness of broken edges (metals) or flexibility (organic materials). The choice of restoration materials may be limited by the potential reactivity of the artefact. Ceramic material is robust and inherently very strong. Edges of breaks are often thick, inert and rigid. Provided care is taken with the selection of gapfill material and method of application, then restoration can be carried out without putting the object at risk. The use of detachable fills limits the amount of work which needs be carried out in contact with the object (Koob 1987). Confining the painting to the gapfill negates problems of staining or contamination from this source. Ceramic material is, therefore, amenable to restoration. Techniques can be applied which will least affect the cultural 'properties', and materials can be used which are easily and completely removable without hazard to any original parts (IIC-Canadian Group 1986). Thus restoration is achievable within the conservators' professional ethics in terms of the safety of the object (AIC 1994; UKIC 1983). The onus must then fall on the curators and designers of a gallery to give justifiable reasons as to why the restoration of an object is necessary.

The British Museum has nearly 100 galleries (British Museum 1991b), the majority of which house permanent exhibitions. Each permanent gallery is carefully designed to a set house style. The gallery has to have a 'story' based on the academic intent and purpose of the exhibition, and set within an historical and geographical context. The story of the gallery is illustrated by the objects and reinforced by relevant graphics, information panels, labels and photographs. The objects, therefore, are the core of the display, and how the ceramics will be presented will depend upon their contribution to the 'story', which will reflect the period and culture represented in the display.

The Museum's collections which illustrate early cultures have mostly been recovered through archaeological excavation. Here the artefacts are viewed as data, and are the primary source of information on past human activity. The paucity of preserved, or recovered, material and lack of historical documentation limits information which can be presented to the public. Early galleries tend to be represented by diagnostic pottery which can be used to identify particular periods, stages of technological development or discrete cultural groups. Aesthetic interpretation of the objects may not be necessary or possible (Johnson 1993). Restoration work for the 'archaeological' galleries, such as the recently opened Egyptian gallery, tends to be minimal. Gap-filling is carried out for support, and, to a lesser extent, to complete the profile of a vessel, but the in-painting is tonal (Buys and Oakley 1993) (Plate 1).

Collections become more extensive in the later classical periods for which there has been greater preservation of material and historical information exists. In these circumstances it may be possible to establish, in far greater detail, the original cultural importance of the objects and even sometimes identify ceramics that were conceived as 'works of art'. Such objects have exceptional intrinsic value which it is essential to define clearly. To the curators of these collections, the value of restorative approaches is increased.

Greek red and black figure ware was, and is, highly valued, not only for the skills of the potter, but also for the skills of the painter (Williams 1985; Noble 1988). In such cases the ceramic has importance in itself, but it is also a 'canvas' on which another work of art has been painted. Restoration within the British Museum classical ceramic collections therefore increases in terms of the level of filling and painting which is undertaken. Most gaps will be filled to complete the form of the vessel and the painting will imitate the reflective qualities of the ceramic finish. Missing areas of design are not inpainted since it would be unethical to interpret areas of loss on free-hand designs. However, for the skill of the painter and the beauty of the scenes to be appreciated, missing areas are filled and painted to the colour of the surrounding ceramic. The visitor can then appreciate the object with the minimum distraction from the restoration (Fisher 1992) (Plates 2, 3).

Within the 'classical' galleries there is a tendency for 'star objects' to be restored to a greater degree than the common wares. In some cases this is justified, especially if the object is of primary importance to the gallery. However, since the information presented to the viewer is so dependant upon the appearance of the objects, disparity in the level of restoration can lead to a misrepresentation of the importance of an object within a culture. This is counter to the ethics of both curators and conservators as it reflects the opinions of the present rather than accurately representing the past (Museums Association 1982). A common gallery policy on the levels of restoration minimises this problem.

Temporary exhibitions within the British Museum do not necessarily follow the house style. They can be used to display a newly acquired collection, to record the work of an antiquity department in a particular area, or to coincide with a 'celebration' or a conference on a particular subject (British Museum 1991b). Where exhibitions are put on to show the finest examples of ceramic wares from a culture, they can be viewed as art exhibitions. Some recently collected, contemporary Japanese ceramics, were made as works of art; should they go on display they would be presented in this context. Modern collections of art objects are generally in pristine condition, but historical art objects may need to be restored. In such an exhibition the aim is not to show the objects as they have survived today but rather as they would have been seen and valued within their culture. In the Italian Maiolica exhibition of 1987 (Wilson 1987) the material was restored to make the repair as invisible as possible. Here restoration is at its most extreme. Gaps and chips were filled to restore the surface of the objects to their original, undamaged appearance. This temporary exhibition, which was displayed for only three months took over six years of conservation time to prepare. This can be considered an acceptable use of time if one considers the cultural impact that such creative art has, which is demonstrated by its ability to provide a source of reference and inspiration for subsequent artistic developments (Stransky 1978) (Plate 4). In fact, this exhibition was more akin to an exhibition of easel paintings than to an exhibition of pottery.

Within an 'Art' exhibition, colour matching imitates the original surface, in terms of tone, reflectance, and, in the case of porcelain, translucency. Designs are inpainted in all but the largest areas of loss. The presence and extent of the restoration and reconstruction is detectable, but it is not conspicuous (IIC-Canadian Group 1986; Oddy 1992) (Plate 5).

RESTORATION - IS IT ACCEPTABLE?

The variety of galleries and range of objects within the British Museum's collection, have, therefore, to be considered when restoration is to take place. There can be no set policy for a level of restoration in a museum which can be seen as an 'art' as well as an 'archaeological' museum (Hodges 1975). The decision to restore must be a team effort, involving the designer, who knows the 'story' of the gallery, the curator, who has detailed knowledge of the object and its cultural significance, and the conservator who can assess the stability of the object and its potential for restoration (Corfield 1988).

Curators in the British Museum are recruited to specialise in specific cultures or periods and most become world experts within their field of study. They can produce comparative objects or historical references if a decision is made to restore an object. When justified reasons are backed up by accurate reference material, restoration in the context of British Museum galleries can be seen as acceptable.

However, a conservator has other responsibilities to the British Museum's collections beyond the preparation of objects for display. Conserving all objects to a level where they are in a stable condition, with good storage conditions to ensure that they are preserved for future generations, should be the primary concern.

The amount of time which is presently allocated to preparing objects for display is disproportionately and unacceptably high in comparison with that available for conservation of the study collections. This is a problem for many museums where emphasis has to be placed on the 'public face' to attract much needed support in terms of sponsorship, grants and donations. The galleries are maintained and temporary exhibitions changed on a regular basis. When grants or sponsorship are secured it is often with a proviso that work will be completed within a set, and often short, period of time. Sponsorship is rarely given for 'behind the scenes' work, and so improvements in the storage conditions and work on the reference collections has to be fitted in around the constant demand for high levels of work for the galleries.

With the current economic and political climate, this situation is unlikely to change in the foreseeable future. Museums, such as the British Museum, will become more and more dependant on private revenue, which in return will expect 'public' recognition of its contributions. The demands for conservation of objects for the galleries will therefore increase. It is up to museum conservators to find a way to redress the balance and provide ourselves with more time for the conservation of the study collections.

Most conservators now work within a policy of minimum intervention. This is the ideal approach to the conservation of objects for storage, but it is not always appropriate to display situations. As the purpose of restoring an object is to extend the visual information that it presents it must be accepted that a degree of restoration is necessary within the display context.

To restore to a level of the Egyptian galleries could be seen as the optimum compromise. However, this may well detract from the viewers appreciation of some of the museums objects.

What must be concentrated on instead is achieving the minimum amount of restoration within a particular gallery context. It is the conservators responsibility to try to influence decisions made about the level of restoration in a gallery; to question the need for, and extent of, the work; to determine if restoration really will extend the information beyond that already apparent from the un-restored object. Conservators must guard against the wish of the curator to present the object as 'perfect' just because this has been acceptable in the past and because this can be easily and safely achieved for ceramic objects.

Having established the need for restoration, conservators must then safeguard against carrying out work to a level which is more reflective of their desire to present conservation skills to the public than a realistic evaluation of the needs of the object. If tonal inpainting of the gap-fill does not detract from the aesthetic qualities of the object, then close colour matching should not be suggested.

There will be resistance to such a change in policy; curators have been presented with objects which have been extensively filled and closely painted for much of the British Museum's history. To move away from this 'restore-all' attitude will have to be a gradual process, with the aim of not stopping the restoration but of cutting out all the unnecessary extremes.

The curators in the British Museum care deeply for the objects under their guardianship; they, like conservators, can no longer see display as separate from the care of the collections as a whole. Conservators must encourage them to take a more holistic approach, to appreciate that extensive conservation time spent on preparing objects for display means that these resources are not available for the maintenance of the study collections.

Compromises are beginning to occur; the level of restoration for 'archaeological' galleries and 'secondary' galleries (areas which were formerly storage rooms but which have now been opened to the public) has been significantly reduced.

Such compromises may, however, never be reached for the objects in the temporary 'art' exhibitions because of the very nature of this type of display. However, conservators could move some way towards reducing restoration if they can, with other members of the gallery team, re-emphasise, or even redefine, the objectives to which all are working. If restoration can be achieved within the overall context of the needs of each object in the collection then it can be considered that restoration for display is acceptable.

Finally, and most importantly, all conservation work must be recorded to assist future conservators who may have to dismantle these restorations. Furthermore, the health and safety of future conservators must be borne in mind when selecting the materials. It is important to avoid, as far as possible, future generations of conservators being subjected to the types of solvents and treatments required today to undo the work of the past.

REFERENCES

American Institute For Conservation, 1994. Code of Ethics and Standards of Practice. in *Directory*, 21-34. The American Institute for Conservation of Historic and Artistic Works, Washington

British Museum Design Office, 1991a. *A Curators' Guide to Planning Exhibitions*. London

British Museum Design Office, 1991b. *A Users' Guide to the House Style*. London

Bushell, S.W. 1977. *Chinese Pottery and Porcelain*. Oxford

Buys, S. and Oakley, V. 1993. *The Conservation and Restoration of Ceramics*. 119-48, Oxford

Corfield, M. 1988. Towards a Conservation Profession. *Conservation Today* (Preprints for the UKIC 30th Anniversary Conference) (ed. V. Todd), 4-8. London

Cronyn, J. 1980. The Potential of Archaeological Conservation. in *Conservation, Archaeology and Museums*, UKIC Occasional Paper **1**, 8-9

Cronyn, J. 1990. *The Elements of Archaeological Conservation*, 141-53. London

Fisher, P.G. 1992. The Sophilos Vase. in *The Art of the Conservator* (ed. A. Oddy) 163-76. London

Hodges, H. 1975. Problems and ethics of the Restoration of Pottery. in *Conservation in Archaeology and the Applied Arts* (ed. D. Leigh *et al*), 37-8. IIC, London

Johns, C. 1986. The Roman Silver Cups from Hockwold, Norfolk. *Archaeologia*, **108**, 2-13

Johnson, J. 1993. Conservation and Archaeology in Great Britain and the United States: A Comparison. *Journal of the American Institute for Conservation*, **32**, 249-69

Koob, S. 1987. Detachable Plaster Restoration for Archaeological Ceramics. *Recent Advances in Conservation and Analysis of Artifacts* (compiled by J. Black) (University of London, Institute of Archaeology, Jubilee Conservation Conference), 63-6, London

Museums Association, 1982. *Code of Conduct for Museum Curators: draft*. London

Needham, S. 1980. An assemblage of Late Bronze Age Metalworking Debris from Dainton, Devon. *Proceedings of the Prehistoric Society*, **46**, 177-215

Noble, J.V. 1988. *The techniques of Painted Attic Pottery*. (2nd ed.) London

Oddy, W.A. and Holmes, R. 1992. The Hockwold Treasure. in *The Art of the Conservator* (ed. A. Oddy), 137-50. London

Oddy, W.A. 1992. Introduction. in *The Art of the Conservator* (ed. A. Oddy), 7-12. London

Olive, J. and Pearson, C. 1975. The Conservation of ceramics from marine archaeological sources. in *Conservation in Archaeology and the Applied Arts* (ed. D. Leigh *et al*) 63-8. IIC, London

Sawle, J. 1983-4. Ceramic salt-making debris from Droitwich. *Bulletin of the Experimental Firing Group*, **2**, 5-12

Sparkes, B.A. 1981. *Greek Pottery: an Introduction*, 1-20. Manchester

Stransky, Z. 1978. The problems of contents, didactics, and aesthetics of modern museum exhibitions. in *Museological Principles of Museum Exhibitions*, 78-82. Institute of Conservation and Methodology, Hungary

United Kingdom Institute for Conservation, 1983. *Guidance for Conservation Practice.*

Ward, C., Sully, D. and Lee, J. 1992. Conservation of Waterlogged Bark Bowls. *Newsletter* ICOM Working Group For Wet Organic Archaeological Materials **23,** 8-9

Williams, D. 1985. *Greek Vases.* London

Wilson, T. 1987. *Ceramic Art of the Italian Renaissance.* London

Wilson, D.M. 1989a. *The Collections of the British Museum.* London

Wilson, D.M. 1989b. *The British Museum, Purpose and Politics.* London

Plate 1   Nubian Jar reconstructed for display in the Early Egypt Gallery. This is an archaeological gallery and gap filling is minimal.

Plate 5   A sixteenth-century Chinese vase which had been damaged around the shoulder area. The gap was filled and closely colour matched but inpainting of the surface decoration was restricted to the border design. The tree was not inpainted.

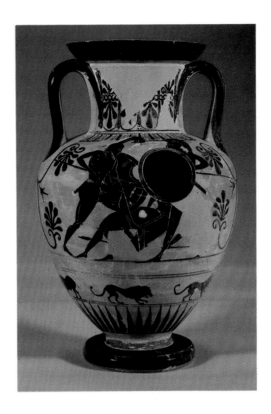

Plate 2   Greek Attic amphora 500 BC completely filled with tonal inpainting to imitate the ground colour of the vessel for a 'classical' gallery

Plate 3   Late seventeenth-century, south-east Iranian, glazed plate filled and inpainted with a neutral tone Emphasis is placed on the reflective qualities of the paint finish.

Plate 4   A sixteenth-century Italian maiolica plate which had been chipped and broken. Areas are filled and closely colour matched for a temporary 'Art' exhibition.